COMICS

In 1982 John Connor was a young sketch writer, stand-up and freelance journalist. Crap at all three, he decided while compering a show and watching a performer crack jokes with a paper bag over his head that comedy might be very silly but as nobody else was going to write about it he would. He started the cabaret section in *City Limits* and now writes about comedy and theatre for the national Press including the *Guardian*, the *Independent*, *The Times* and *The Stage*. He is also a regular pundit and produces comedy pieces for LBC.

COMICS

*A Decade of Comedy
at the Assembly Rooms*

John Connor

Foreword by Arthur Smith

PAPERMAC

First published in 1990 by
PAPERMAC
a division of Macmillan Publishers Limited
4 Little Essex Street London WC2R 3LF
and Basingstoke

Associated companies in Auckland, Delhi, Dublin, Gaborone,
Hamburg, Harare, Hong Kong, Johannesburg, Kuala Lumpur,
Lagos, Manzini, Melbourne, Mexico City, Nairobi, New York,
Singapore and Tokyo

ISBN 0-333-54171-5

A CIP catalogue record for this book
is available from the British Library

Printed by Butler and Tanner Ltd, Frome, Somerset

ACKNOWLEDGEMENTS

William Burdett-Coutts and Philippa Johnston of Assembly Theatre Limited, Addison Cresswell of Off The Kerb
Productions, Gordon Dean of *The Scotsman*, Loretta Sacco of Talkback and Susanna Wadeson of Macmillan London
Limited.

In memory of Jack, whose clowning days
were the best years of his life.

The author would like to thank all the performers who
readily gave up their time to be interviewed and whose
story this is. Thanks also to the intrepid Malcolm Hay, who
flew up to Edinburgh in a hurricane and dug out the
research material – truly the Indiana Jones of cabaret.

Foreword to the Foreword

(Phone rings eight times.)

Arthur : Hello.

Ed. : Hello, Arthur. Listen, we're commissioning a book about the last ten years of the Edinburgh Festival . . .

Arthur : Do you realise what the time is?

Ed. : It's based around the Assembly Rooms . . .

Arthur : I said, 'Do you know what time it is?'

Ed. : Yes, it's about midday.

Arthur : Is it? Oh.

Ed. : Would you write the foreword to it?

Arthur : Good God, no. (Pause.) Why me?

Ed. : Well apart from Brian Patten-McGough, you've performed at it more often than anyone else. Besides, Griff Rhys Jones said no.

Arthur : But some posh book about the Edinburgh Festival is an appalling idea.

Ed. : You don't like the idea?

Arthur : It is the antithesis of the spirit of the Edinburgh Fringe.

Ed. : Does that mean anything?

Arthur : Probably not.

Ed. : Good, well write that then. And stick a couple of jokes in.

Arthur : Can I write it in the form of a Socratic dialogue?

Ed. : I doubt it. Can you?

Arthur : What about a phone conversation then?

Ed. : Well, only at the beginning. People get bored with reading dialogue.

Opposite: *Arthur Smith (1984)*

Arthur : Oh, all right then. I'll drift into prose.

One year I am an exciting new comic actor, acclaimed and applauded, the next I am a shagged-out has-been, pitied and derided

I've written a foreword to my foreword because I am fearful I may not be able to fulfil expectations of what a foreword should be. I assume it comprises a few vague homilies and anecdotes which invite the reader to enjoy the agreeable feast to come. Usually the article is headed by a smudged photo of its author, a mayor or some distantly remembered actor. I suppose I at least fit that category, since I am an ex-mayor of Balham.

A book like this is in danger of being twee, bland, formal, boring, well designed, unpretentious, expensive and predictable. Shows at the Edinburgh Fringe, on the other hand, are twee, bland, formal, boring, well designed, unpretentious, expensive and predictable – sometimes. More often they are chaotic, extreme, anarchic, exciting, badly designed, pretentious, cheap, unpredictable and pretty well any other description you want to dream up. Perhaps the only adjective that could never be applied to the Edinburgh Fringe is 'healthy'. Even that's not true, since the word could happily describe the amount of money a few people earn from it.

I have written shows for the Edinburgh Festival, though at the end of August I invariably find that in fact the shows have written me. One year I am an exciting new comic actor, acclaimed and applauded, the next I am a shagged-out has-been, pitied and derided. I have performed in Edinburgh to large audiences of appreciative TV executives, and I have also done shows where the entire audience was my earnest and slightly dim cousin Kevin. These extremes are even possible in the same evening. I once went from a TV recording at STV where I was cosseted by make-up girls and assistant floor managers, to a pub round the corner inhabited by tripping punks – one of whom poured a pint of his piss over me.

But then having a pint of piss poured over you is more interesting than lying on a beach reading a Robert Ludlum novel and that is why I have pitched up in Edinburgh twelve out of the last thirteen Augusts. (The one I missed was due to an ill-fated love affair, started at the previous Festival.) In February someone always asks me if I'm going that year, and I always say no because I can't tolerate the prospect of the stress, the cold bum, the unfamiliar lodgings, the rubbish I talk, the hangovers, the hoarse voice, the unwashed socks. Then over the next few weeks I realise I have an idea for a show and, well, Edinburgh is a good place to try something new, isn't it? Everyone else will be there. What else will I be doing? What will I put in the Fringe programme?

I realise that I write this from the perspective of a full-time performer. I am not skint any more either. The Fringe is more truly represented by the schoolgirl who puts on a musical with her mates, the intense under-graduate who wants to write plays and has written a very bad first one, the South African actor with a story to tell, the aspiring comic who hopes to get a couple of gigs and a fuck, or the local shopkeeper who develops an unexpected interest in Russian experimental theatre.

It's difficult to imagine how a book can do justice to this arty orgy. Of course there are threads to be found, careers to be charted, jokes to be recalled, disasters to be laughed at, and some good old pictures of famous actors with silly haircuts and flared trousers, but if I were asked to write such a book I would do it in the form of a picaresque novel or else a folder stuffed full of strange memorabilia and blotchy A4 hand-outs.

Frankly, my foreword to my foreword's not going terribly well, is it? (*No* – Ed.)

Opposite: Arthur Smith (1984)

FOREWORD

The Edinburgh Festival is a wonderful event. The greatest Arts Festival in the West, it attracts writers, painters, actors, musicians from all over the world. Every August Edinburgh (surely the most dramatic city in Britain) provides a platform for exciting, original and creative work of every conceivable kind, from low-brow comedy to great classics, from pavement art to full-scale symphonies. So I was thrilled to be asked to write the foreword to this book. What a brilliant idea to capture ten years of it in one luxurious volume. (*This is more like it* – Ed.) And it is entirely appropriate to centre on the magnificent Assembly Rooms in George Street, home to so many great performances.

It has been my great privilege to know the author of this book and to have spent time discussing art with him in Edinburgh. He has dealt with the subject with the panache and flair he usually reserves only for smashing balls around the ground for the *New Statesman* Cricket Team. (And if he's slipped in that business about the chip shop then I shall be contacting my solicitor.)

So, dear reader, enjoy, enjoy.

Ed. :   Yeah, well, that's the sort of thing.

Arthur :   I'll send it off this evening.

Ed. :   O K. You going to Edinburgh this year?

Arthur :   No.

Arthur Smith
Balham
February 1990

Opposite: *The Assembly Rooms*

INTRODUCTION

If you want to get your first TV series before you're thirty, put together a comedy set and get out there. It helps if you're funny but if you're not it isn't necessarily a handicap

It takes a lot of guts to be a stand-up comic. There's no one up on stage with you to save your soul if things go wrong, no one to blame but yourself, and, at the beginning of your career, there's the prospect of only being able to afford to go home on the bus. All you can do is tuck yourself up on the back seat in the foetal position and hope that no one notices you've been reduced to sucking your thumb in public.

On the other hand, if you survive the hard times there may well be good ones ahead. At the beginning of the eighties it wasn't exactly a career move to become a comic – now, ironically it can be looked upon as a serious occupation.

At the start of the nineties, there is a comedy boom on both sides of the Atlantic, and even further a sea down in Australia. The English-speaking world has an inter-connected comedy circuit – international festivals in Montréal and Melbourne – and bookings are possible world-wide. In addition, television, the preying media shark of the stand-up (you have to get in the water; you want to get bitten for the publicity; you just hope you don't lose one of your limbs in the process) is fast catching up and developing this new market. In the States, for example, cable channels HBO and MTV have both launched their own full-time comedy schedules, while in Britain if you want to get your first TV series before you're thirty, put together a comedy set and get out there. It helps if you're funny but if you're not it isn't necessarily a handicap. The big thing is the ability to take the ego knocks and keep going.

Once you've cracked it the best means of enhancing your career is to wangle your way somehow to the Edinburgh Fringe Festival. Unless you're relatively well known it's likely to be a costly experience – so be resourceful, like London-based comic Dreenagh Darrel who last year got into a double bill with a young act whose brother had a flat in the city.

For three weeks of the year Edinburgh crawls with comics, light entertainment producers from TV, radio and stage and agents/managers. It's become like a sales conference – a veritable Comedy Trade Industry. It's the motor show: find out who are the best runners, the nippiest performers, the best investment. You'll get everything from the smooth Rolls Royce of acts, which purrs along luxuriously like the dream winner it is, to the clapped-out old banger whom everyone has written off but who may well rise to prove they were going to be classic models all along. As yet there has not been enough time for the latter to happen in Edinburgh, but one day it will. Jackie Mason, the American-Jewish Borscht Belt comic, is now a major star – yet the style that had him become a forgettable sixties' act has hardly changed a jot.

A trade fair will only last a week, a conference a few days; at the Edinburgh Festival hundreds of comedy performers are squeezed into one place for three weeks. All those egos fighting for space! If you've got

Being a masochist is an essential part of a comic's nature

a successful show you'll be having a good time; a bad show and each day you will feel like a child waiting for the next day's promised punishment at school. You'll do anything to get out of it, but be there you will – day after day after day.

Comics are a very sociable breed. Maybe it's because doing an act is such a lonely experience that they feel a need to commune with their fellow performers. But whatever the reason, flock together they do. Over the years a stand-up has moved from being a rare bird to being one of a pigeon pack that seemingly will never go away. Each year they choose a roost after a few days, and from then on the bar in question will never be quite the same. In recent years it's been the Gilded Balloon – a new venue that has sought to rival the Assembly Rooms for the strongest comedy at the Festival. Into a small bar some thirty feet long and never more than six feet across the whole small world of comedy squeezes itself to have a good time. Being a masochist is another essential part of a comic's nature.

While the social side has got wilder, comedy at the Festival over the last ten years has become more professional. The Edinburgh Fringe hasn't caused this, it is only a repository for what is happening in the country and, to an extent, internationally. In the eighties the growth art form of live theatre was undoubtedly stand-up comedy – and this was reflected at the Festival. It has been described as a comedy highjack, but the change in emphasis is no different from that of the university revues of the mid-fifties which culminated in 1960 in *Beyond the Fringe*. The grouping of Oxbridge-graduate revue performers Peter Cook, Dudley Moore, Alan Bennett and Jonathan Miller formed a hegemony that was to last (neatly for the purposes of this book) until just about the time the Assembly Rooms were opened in 1981.

The Assembly Rooms were an immediate hit. Groups paid for their own space and the Assembly took care of press and publicity. Now, at the start of a new decade, they have become something of an unofficial official Fringe Festival. Once you are in the Assembly Rooms you are considered to have made it, and although playing there doesn't guarantee any show to be a hit, even duff ones can usually get by.

As the fortunes of comedy have risen so has its profile at the Assembly Rooms. There have, of course, been plenty of other things going on – and some of these we'll touch on – but the centre of this book will be a look at the comics that have played there. How has the Edinburgh Festival been for them? And how has it helped, or hindered, their various careers?

Overleaf: *The Assembly Rooms*

3

MOVING PICTURE MIME SHOW
OLEH
TOBY SEDGWICK, PAUL FILIPIAK & DAVID GAINES

In the beginning William Burdett-Coutts was a drama student at Essex. In 1979 he wanted to put on a play at the Edinburgh Fringe but couldn't afford it. 'So I took over a venue – the Harry Younger Hall – and sub-let. I put on three shows – acted in one, directed another and produced a third.'

A few months earlier, on 19 May to be precise, the Comedy Store opened at a strip club in London's Soho. There had not been a regular comedy club in London since the decline of the satire boom in the early sixties and the demise of Peter Cook's club, The Establishment. Strangely enough, the new site was literally round the corner from the old one. While Coutts was operating as an entrepreneurial amateur a whole new milieu was about to explode within the performing arts, but at that point you'd never have thought that the two, within a few years, would be working together.

By 1981 Coutts was looking for a venue and asked the council if he could have the one room in the Assembly Rooms complex that the official Festival had decided not to use.

Coutts: 'To my surprise they offered me the entire building. I was a production manager at the Old Vic at the time, and I sat at the back of the stalls organising the event without a penny and just an old type-writer. In terms of the programme it was a matter of what one could get. It also happened extraordinarily fast. It was all put together in just six weeks. It was very exciting and crazy.'

In 1981 the most famous person to appear at the Assembly Rooms was Griff Rhys Jones as one member of Comic Business, who were presenting a revue entitled *An Evening Without*. Rory Bremner, who was something of a local *aficionado* of comedy revues at the time, thought perhaps 'the "without" bit was because Rowan Atkinson wasn't in it. I'd seen a good 50 per cent of the material in earlier shows.' At the time Rhys Jones was referred to in the Press as the 'fourth member of the *Not the Nine O'Clock News* team whose name nobody could remember'. But then again, no one had heard of the others he was appearing with at all – Clive Anderson, Jimmy Mulville, Rory McGrath (both *Who Dares Wins* and *Chelmsford 123*) and Martin Bergman.

Rhys Jones: 'I have to say I don't remember much about it. It was the general opinion that I wasn't that well known a member of the *Not* team. Partly because Pamela had certain charms, and Rowan was the curious one. The photographers would always pick on them, which is why Mel and I were thrown together.

'I slipped into doing *Not* because the producer, John Lloyd, was an old mate of mine. We were BBC Radio Light Entertainment producers

'In terms of the programme it was a matter of what one could get. It also happened extraordinarily fast'

Opposite: *The Moving Picture Mime Show* (1981)

together and had both been in Footlights. He put me in playing the odd milkman or policeman. Then when Chris Langham and he didn't see eye to eye over things I got promoted.

'*An Evening Without* got its name because we were advertising it as a show without a whole range of famous people in it. In fact it was strung together round four years of pleasing turns we'd done in various Footlight shows. It was the sort of stuff you do as a student and don't actually have the balls to do again. Like a song about cow-poking. It was loud, crazy and had lots of rude words and went down well with the audience. But not with the Press.

'Actually, I still turn some of it out in charity shows – and there's nothing like it. It goes down a storm. I actually think you try to recreate as a comedian the earliest stuff you did on stage for the rest of your career.

'Predictably the Press tore us apart, but I met someone in a fruit shop who loved the show and said, "You know that review in *The Scotsman*? My husband wrote that – but I don't agree with it at all." '

'It was the sort of stuff you do as a student and don't actually have the balls to do again. Like a song about cow-poking'

Griff Rhys Jones admits having a TV name was enough to make sure the show sold out: 'We actually made some money out of playing Edinburgh, which I suppose up to then you weren't really expected to do.' But he wasn't the character of the year, nor indeed were any of the other comics . . .

Festivals have their own rhythm and a life which is an amalgam of everyone participating. Even if you're an old hand you cannot help but be swept along by the adrenalin, the meeting of old friends and equally old enemies – and, as is the way of such things, one year's mate can just as easily turn into next year's antagonist. Always in the excitement a few individuals stand out. In this case the award for, to use an American football expression, MVP (Most Valuable Prat) goes to Zack Matalon, who claimed to be a Broadway producer and turned up with his new musical *Light Years Away* to play the Music Hall, the Assembly's biggest venue.

Coutts: 'I was passed him by another producer as a new musical which was to go into Broadway. The cast was his family and on the way up here their minivan broke down. As it was night-time he got them in front of the van's lights and had them rehearsing on the hard shoulder while they were waiting for the AA to turn up.

'He couldn't understand having no audience, and developed a conspiracy theory for why nobody was turning up. If you're heading that way, Edinburgh can really make you flip. I think at one time Zack was trying to sue most people in the building. Indeed what was happening was that his show was becoming something of a cult and all the performers would slip into the back to laugh at it. I seem to remember things getting out of hand and eggs being thrown at Zack. I'm not sure by whom – but Rory McGrath was certainly getting into a feud with him. In fact our chief lawyer came in to see the show and got splattered with eggs. I think Zack at that point ran off stage and got into a fight with his tormentor.'

'If you're heading that way, Edinburgh can really make you flip'

8

Rhys Jones: 'I remember this Zack person was trying all the time to recruit people into his show as, not surprisingly, his cast kept leaving him. I think some of the trouble was caused by us following his show on the same stage. There was lots of tormenting going on – but there was always angst when someone has to take over a stage. In fact Rory and Jimmy [Mulville] have never had suitable relationships with other people in Edinburgh. A few years before they had to decorate a lorry to put it in the Festival parade and they had nothing to do it with. But they found a large quantity of silver paper at a venue called St Mary's. They covered the lorry with it, put a band on top of it and went off to the parade. When they got back they discovered a distraught Phil Pope of the Oxford Revue group – angry to say the least as this silver paper was all they had for their set.

'In the seventies it wasn't a pro festival at all – except for Billy Connolly. I seem to remember something like Manchester University bringing up an undiscovered play called *The Bald Prima Donna* and making up for not getting audiences by putting on a late-night revue called *Death on the Toilet* by a duo calling themselves 20th Century Coyote. We all went to see that. [As this was the beginning of Rik Mayall and Ade Edmondson's double act it is not so surprising.]

'Now it's a career move to be a hit in Edinburgh. It's got so huge it could become a separate community. All it needs is some manufacturing base – cups or something to finance it – and then everyone in the community can entertain everyone else.'

In 1981, *An Evening Without* was something Comic Business ran as much for themselves as for anybody else – an ethos like that of amateur sport. It was not the winning but the taking part that counted. This was about to change.

Rhys Jones: 'We used to do this dreadful "Breakfast Cereal Blues", with terrible music and even more terrible lyrics. The thing that made it funny was that people played bits of breakfast equipment. It was like the crudest panto in the lowest theatre in the land and it got wails of laughter. It amused us – and it amused the audience. By the end of the run the sketch finished up with us covering the audience with cornflakes. It was just a bunch of mates getting together. In fact we were touring the show well before Alternative Cabaret [the first touring new-wave comedy group] started doing so. The idea was to turn up and perform in what you were wearing. Which was quite fortunate with Clive Anderson who, as a practising barrister, was always the last to arrive. At the Derby Playhouse he heard his cue as soon as he got into the back of the theatre and walked straight on stage still wearing his coat and carrying his briefcase!'

Clive Anderson had been one of the first to jump into the stand-up scene. A former Footlights president (1975), he went along to the first night of the Comedy Store.

'I've only done twelve jokes in my life whether I've done stand-up or revue'

*A*nderson: 'It was by accident really but it was nice and challenging. It seemed to consist of groups of young men on beer, which was fine for me as I only do one-line jokes. I could get a laugh in before they were at me. In fact I've only done twelve jokes in my life whether I've done stand-up or revue. If I try a new one out it fails, so I go back to the old stuff. There was no way I was going to develop a big act. Still the Store did make you quite quick on your feet.'

Quick enough for his witty repartee to make him a TV personality years later hosting *Whose Line Is It Anyway?* on Channel 4, and then, inevitably, his own talk show.

Edinburgh wasn't a make-or-break show for any of the *Evening Without* crew – their contacts had already been established at university. It was the new-wavers of cabaret who would benefit. They were not only going to develop stand-up comedy into a pure art form for the first time in this country, they were also in the process of putting together a hierarchy that would eventually take over light entertainment and make it fashionable. A new rock 'n' roll of jokes and slapstick was arriving fast.

*T*he critical comedy hit of that year's Festival was the Alternative Cabaret show with Tony Allen, Jim Barclay, Andy de la Tour and Pauline Melville – four highly political comics who had developed out of the seventies' radical fringe theatre, and then gone on to be the early players at the Comedy Store and the nascent London cabaret circuit. They were, in fact, connected to Comic Business – Martin Bergman, one of the *An Evening Without* performers, was actually producing the Alternative Cabaret show.

*T*ony Allen, who is these days fondly referred to as the 'Grandfather of Alternative Cabaret' doesn't remember much of that particular show, but he does remember Bergman. 'I went round to his flat and he was staying in these flash apartments while he'd put us into a hovel.' A few years later in 1984 Allen was to get revenge on Bergman in passing. Bergman had brought over a trio of American comics under the generic title of New York Stand-Up Comedy – one of whom, Rita Rudner, he was eventually to marry.

Opposite: *Andy de la Tour (1983)*

Overleaf: *Griff Rhys Jones (1981)*

*A*llen: 'One of the male acts was a Jewish comic [Larry Amoros] doing the "Who's that you're with and how much did you pay for her?" routine off the audience. All that horrible stuff. He used to work his way across the front row and I purposefully sat down right at the end where he'd finish. Eventually he came up to me and said, "What do you do?" I replied, "I'm a comedian. What do you do?"'

Allen left the show at that point to applause — and was to be congratulated by the rest of the comic community in the Festival.

In 1981 there wasn't a comic community as such. Coutts says: 'My recollection of the time was that people didn't know each other. There wasn't really a comedy circuit — Alternative Cabaret was kind of it.' The Oxbridge revue versus Alternative Cabaret rivalry was as yet a thing of the future. Tony Allen recalls, 'We did take the Oxbridge mob on at a game of football but Arthur Smith was on our side and he was in a revue at the time. It was all pretty yahoo really. A thinking person's Butlins.'

Of course there had been fighting over the comic cake in the past. Helen Atkinson-Wood of Radioactive only half-jokes when she recalls, 'When I was up in Edinburgh in seventy-seven doing a show with Rowan Atkinson there seemed to be some sort of physical violence on a daily basis. There was a real fizz between Oxford and Cambridge. But then everyone mellowed into hearty lunches and became TV and radio producers, becoming heavily bonded and seamless, giving each other jobs all the time.'

Radioactive had come up to Edinburgh on the back of their success as a BBC radio comedy show. Developing from the Oxford Theatre Group they had been given their opportunity by Jimmy Mulville in his role as a radio producer. He was a former Cambridge boy!

The chaos and madness of the first year of the Assembly Rooms was summed up not in the actions of a performer, but in those of an artisan of quite another ilk. Coutts tells the story of a thief who got lost in the roof of the Assembly Rooms: 'There used to be a flat at the top of the building for the theatre manager. The thief stuck a foot through the skylight of the flat right above the bed — the manager's wife was lying in it at the time. He got stuck and we eventually found him lying in a pool of blood.'

But this wasn't quite as gory as the discovery of a corpse in the building — a diabetic who had supposedly drunk a bottle of whisky. Coutts thinks it was found after a Radioactive performance, but cast member Helen Atkinson-Wood doesn't recall it, though 'there was a rumour going round . . .'

'It was all pretty yahoo really. A thinking person's Butlins'

1982 wasn't exactly a brilliant year for comedy, and stand-up was especially thin on the ground. In fact the only proper example was John Dowie, a comic who pre-dated the Comedy Store by many years and who had been creating his own space by playing fringe theatres. Unlike Connolly, Mike Harding, and his fellow Birmingham performer Jasper Carrott, Dowie hadn't developed out of the folk scene. He really was a comic alone. Sadly he now seems to be going through one of his 'packing in comedy' moods. In fact I've a feeling it might be terminal, which is a real pity, as he's certainly one of the great originals. In undoubtedly my shortest interview ever, he told me: 'John, I'm calling you back as a mate, but I don't want to have anything to do with a book about comedy. I don't remember anything about Edinburgh – except I hated it.' (Fortunately Dowie is himself remembered by many as a major Festival character and crops up in various stories over the decade. No book on the Festival would be complete without a few of Dowie's antics.)

In fact right across the board the Festival was short of things on the light-hearted front. Victoria Wood was up with her recent West End show; buskers Pookiesnackenburger were presenting their best ever musical comedy revue at the Little Lyceum, and the Greatest Show On Legs were cashing in on their balloon dance of *OTT* fame in the Circuit Tent at the Hole in the Ground.

The concept of medium Doris Stokes in the same brochure as the new-wave radical northern poets is quite extraordinary

At the Assembly Rooms there was some very eclectic programming. The concept of medium Doris Stokes in the same brochure as the new-wave radical northern poets – whose star rose and fell all in the same year – is quite extraordinary. There was also Andrew Newton, who was billed as 'The World's Greatest Hypnotist'. Griff Rhys Jones was working as a radio reporter that year and remembers him well:

'He was great. I went to see him six times. I knew his promoter, indeed Andrew actually put him under, and I've always wondered what sort of a deal you could secure for yourself under those circumstances. I thought Stokes was a fraud, but Andrew wasn't. He put my girlfriend of the time under the influence and stuck her in the hallway of the Assembly Rooms for four hours with a placard round her neck saying she was hypnotised and advertising his show. Afterwards she told me she was perfectly happy to do it and knew what she was doing all the time but she wasn't that sort of person at all – she was usually very prickly. Anyone capable of getting her to do that certainly convinced me.'

Surprisingly the hip New Variety of Poets grouping didn't fare too well. They were plastered all over the *NME* and the Music Press in general that year (one, Seething Wells, later became Steven Wells, an *NME* journalist) but their cool hype obviously didn't endear them to the Festival public. They were not helped by rasta poet Benjamin Zephaniah going home after a few days – a trick he would play again the following year, leaving Simon Fanshawe in the lurch.

The stars of the future were all gathered together in consecutive shifts in the Assembly Ballroom. The year before, the Cambridge Footlights had won the first ever Perrier Award for the best revue on the Edinburgh Fringe. (Later cabaret was to be included in its remit – indeed it allowed itself to expand to meet all the changes that the live arts threw at it in the eighties.) A lot is made of Cambridge, and indeed Oxford, people having an easy ride into show business (over the years it's certainly been the case that they have had an easy ticket to becoming BBC Radio Light Entertainment producers) but you couldn't have got more of a dream cast together – even with the hindsight of today – for *The Cellar Tapes*, which starred Emma Thompson, Hugh Laurie, Stephen Fry and Tony Slattery. Only two members of the cast, Penny Dwyer and Paul Shearer, have not become household names.

Fry, Laurie, Thompson and Shearer returned to the Festival in 1982 with new member, Robert Bathurst, and a revue entitled *A Sense of Nonsense*. They obviously didn't put an extraordinary amount of work into it. *The Scotsman* review picks out Fry and Laurie's 'Shakespeare Masterclass' as their 'brilliant parody' of the evening and a brilliant parody it was too – unfortunately it had also been the star turn of their winning *Cellar Tapes* show. Still, Edinburgh had highlighted them enough to have the pair, along with Emma Thompson, already signed for a new Granada sketch show, which also pulled in the best writer from the world of alternative comedy – Ben Elton. (Elton was employed first as a writer, but when Rik Mayall dropped out of the project, he was promoted to perform in the show.) *Al Fresco* was to launch the next year – though a solid attempt, it never took off. However it would lead to one of the major television light entertainment strands in the eighties: *The Black Adder*.

Ben Elton joined up with Richard Curtis to write the second series of *Black Adder* in 1984. By 1989 with its First World War scenario it was to become the most popular new-wave sitcom for many a million viewers. Not only did it hit the TV top ten, it was that rare thing of modern television – a show appealing to the critics and the general public across all age groups. Its final image of a field of poppies after Black Adder and his crew have been mowed down in a senseless attack, brought a tear to the nation's eye. Not since the great days of the sixties and early seventies had a sitcom reached such heights. Perhaps it worked so well because the smooth and controlled writing of Richard Curtis, who's been the mainstay of Rowan Atkinson's comedy output since their Oxford days, blended so well with Elton's precise but rather maniacal energies. And it didn't hurt any that Atkinson, Fry and Laurie were also superb.

Opposite: *John Dowie (1984)*

The show that followed directly on from the *Nonsense* team starred Jeremy Beadle. If you stayed to see both shows it must have been a bit like switching from BBC2 to LWT

With that as a bench-mark let me take you to the furthest extreme I can possibly think of – and, by some extraordinary chance, it happens to be rooted in fact.

At Edinburgh everybody rubs shoulders with everybody else and the show that followed directly on from the *Nonsense* team starred Jeremy Beadle. He came on at midnight in, considering the hour, an aptly named show: *An Evening in Bed with Jeremy Beadle*. If you stayed to see both shows it must have been a bit like switching from B B C 2 to L W T.

Beadle was already a member of the highly successful – in T V rating terms – *Game for a Laugh* team. By the end of the eighties his *Beadle's About* tricks on the public would, like *Black Adder*, be a top-ten regular. The arts community will always look down on real populist entertainment but it must be remembered that although many people try to create populist grab-those-big-ratings programmes, they often fail. (Many of the successful formats like *Blind Date* are bought in.) Whatever you think of Beadle, he has the knack for creating popular shows.

*B*eadle: 'I was supposed to open at midnight – but as is the way of things being the last show in a theatre with a rolling rostrum of acts on the first night, I went up rather late. 1.15 a.m., to be precise. Now I'm not really a live performer, or any sort of a performer at all – I'm a presenter and a show deviser, but I walked out to an audience of eight people. The trouble was I needed at least nine for the audience participation element of the show. The first thing I said was, "By God, but you're going to be working hard tonight."

'Actually the first time I ever did a live performance was at a Royal Variety Show. I said to the organiser, Lord Delfont, when I came off, "That's the first time I've ever been on stage in my life." He looked at me and said, "Thank the Lord you didn't tell me just before you went on." '

*A*n early co-editor of London listings magazine *Time Out*, Beadle is also a Festival fan.

'The thing about being mainstream in telly terms, like me, is that it doesn't actually put bums on seats at the Festival. And that's what it's all about. Bums on seats'

I catch all the one-man shows I can. You know when you're there, you're at tomorrow and can't spot it. I remember Billy Connolly – I was told to go and see him in 1980 and caught *The Welly Boot Show*. I couldn't understand what everyone was raving about and there I was sitting at the cradle of genius.

'The thing about being mainstream in telly terms, like me, is that it doesn't actually put bums on seats at the Festival. And that's what it's all about. Bums on seats.'

*B*eadle is refreshingly honest about his craft. Along with Mike Smith, he's a major target for stand-ups – do a Beadle joke and you can always get a laugh. How does he take it when he, for a change, is got at?

'I understand it, and actually expect it. I've been at the Hackney Empire [the old music hall now once again operating as a variety theatre in London] and the word has got round that I am in and the jokes start. I don't mind but I actually think it's *passé* – it's going for the easy laugh. Mind you, even I'm slightly embarrassed to be put in the same bracket as Mike Smith.'

The Cambridge crew and Beadle may have been total opposites but there was at least one other show that year, and indeed the year before, that was totally and absolutely original. Ivor Cutler, ex-teacher and cult humorist, goes way back to the sixties and for a while back then was even fêted by Paul McCartney. His stories, poems and songs are a complete world in themselves – his is a gentle surrealism that can have you wafting into hysterics.

These days he refuses to perform out of a 100-mile radius of his home in London: 'So that I can get back to my own bed at night.' So although he is a native Scot it's unlikely that he'll grace any more Festivals. Still, his approach to the Festival when he was there was as original and personal as his art.

Cutler: 'I find it quite exhausting to perform, so I don't go and see any other people's work. Phyliss King [his musical accompanist] and I would go and paint Edinburgh Castle or go and collect shells at Portobello.

'The only difference for me is that I was in one place for two weeks. I remember in eighty-one, it was very hot in the Assembly Rooms, especially when you were performing. Then when you'd leave it would be very cold outside, and I'd get a chill. When I went to my digs I'd wake up in the middle of the night soaked from cold sweats. Oh crumbs, I thought, this was going to be funny – but it's not so funny after all, is it?

'Anyway, later on that year I discovered a homeopathic remedy called *Aconite* – a poisonous flower. And it stops you getting chills. I remember 1982 because with this remedy I had a tolerable time!'

Though it's sometimes difficult to remember in their company, comics are human too. Ivor Cutler is one of those rare, joyful performers who actually isn't putting on an act, he's merely showing a unique character to a wider world. As his fellow Scot Arnold Brown might put it, 'And why not?'

During 1982 the avuncular boss, William Burdett-Coutts found himself getting into the first of many scrapes with some of his acts. There is no worse mix than the headiness of a Festival, artist egos and money.

The Flying Pickets, who were going to be one-and-a-half hit wonders, were made at Edinburgh in 1982. Another team developing out of seventies radical theatre, they first met as actors on the 7:84 musical show about miners, *One Big Blow*. In the back of the van, as they trawled

Overleaf: *Pookiesnackenburger (1982)*

19

up the motorways of Britain's national Fringe theatre circuit, they used to harmonise old songs together. When the tour finished they started working the small London cabaret circuit, singing standards in a very up-beat and theatrical fashion. This bunch of lefty actors were going to reintroduce a cappella as a populist form in this country – there are still innumerable, and to be honest incredibly tame, acts like theirs working the cabaret circuit as a result of their success. From their showcase at the Assembly Rooms they got a tour of Australia and eventually their recording contract.

Coutts: 'I nearly punched a Picket that year. He accused me of fiddling the box office. What really annoyed me was that he was having an affair with the box office manager – I never went in there.'

The following year things didn't improve a lot between them either – the rock 'n' roll ethos had also arrived at the Assembly Rooms. By 1984 musicians were performing either on their way up or, as in the case of Ian Dury, when their careers were in decline.

Coutts: 'Dury had a heavy with him and a journalist tried to get back stage to see him. The journalist got beaten up – or at least punched very badly.'

Music bouncers are obviously a group who don't find Festival high spirits change their morality one iota.

Opposite: *Ivor Cutler (1986)*

Overleaf: *Flying Pickets (1983)*

1983

Of all the years of the decade, 1983 is the dream one. French and Saunders and Rik Mayall, if not quite fully fledged stars, were already well on their way to stardom. They were joined at the Assembly Rooms by Ben Elton, Hale and Pace, John Sessions and, on the American arts culture side, Eric Bogosion. Cliffhanger appeared for a second year with their hilarious sci-fi spoof *They Came from Somewhere Else*. This was soon turned into a Channel 4 series, though it was destined not to transfer to the small screen very well, for low-budget reasons more than anything else. The team have had more TV success recently with their surreal tales of an everyday police station *Morning Sarge* for BBC2. The National Theatre of Brent were by now a major theatrical draw and packing out the Music Hall with their two-man epic *The Messiah*. And that year's Perrier winners, the Australian clowning duo Los Trios Ring-barkus, were also there.

But that wasn't where the fun – or at least the good stories – were. The Festival may have been packed with the stars of the future, but it was also the wildest year of the Edinburgh decade, and everyone I interviewed for this book took me straight back to one instance, and one individual – Malcolm Hardee and his tractor.

Generally, the more famous the comic, the less interesting they are as a person

Generally, the more famous the comic, the less interesting they are as a person. Making it in comedy requires as much, if not more, dedication than any other human endeavour. It's a craft that at times can reach the level of creative art – original jazz comic Lord Buckley and Lenny Bruce were perhaps the nearest to that – but for most it's playing the game and manoeuvring in back rooms. You need the talent, but you also need the motivation to succeed.

Americans Buckley and Bruce were destined never to be more than cult figures – yet they were both highly original, if not touching on genius as artists of stand-up comedy. They were also two wild, crazy guys, who would never fit into the safe showbiz category. Malcolm Hardee certainly doesn't fit into the safe showbiz category, and he's not exactly the world's greatest comic either – though he is probably the world's best con man of comedy. In any case he gets away with an awful lot on stage and off.

For most of the seventies Malcolm Hardee couldn't get out much – spending most of his time in prison. In 1970 he got banged away for three years for stealing Peter Walker's Rolls Royce. Why did he do it?

Opposite: *People Show Cabaret (1982)*
Overleaf left: *Jennifer Saunders (1983)*
Overleaf right: *Dawn French (1983)*

'Well, it had the keys in it. Actually, I crashed it in a ditch and knocked over a telegraph pole. A minute later a police car came round the corner – we ran but didn't get away. The original Bernie the Bolt from *The Golden Shot* was with me – so if you ever wondered why they changed Bernie mid-series now you know. I got three years for that.'

After a further spell for cheque fraud he came out, went straight, and ended up in a touring kids' show. There he met Punch and Judy man Martin Soan and suggested they do a pornographic version for adults. Off they went and toured hippy fairs and open-air pop concerts. He got put away for a third time after this for burglary, though this time he claims he was framed. He was jailed for two years but released on appeal after nine months. As he readily admits guilt to the first two, knowing Malcolm he probably was innocent – but the time did him good:

'While I was in prison that time I wrote the Greatest Show On Legs sketches. When I got out we were booked down at The Tramshed as a replacement team for the Fundation [the group that launched Hale and Pace], along with Rik Mayall and Ade Edmondson. When we finished the manager came up and said come back next week with a new half-hour, it was then that I remembered all the sketches I'd written in prison.'

By 1982 The Legs were a cult act. Indeed they were the only people actually to be made famous by Chris Tarrant's attempt, with *OTT*, to market *Tiswas* to an adult audience. (Both Alexei Sayle and Lenny Henry had to spend the next few years getting their profiles and careers back into shape.) The Legs, with their infamous nude cha-cha dance, with balloons held in strategic positions, had in three minutes secured for themselves careers for at least the next three years. (Clive James raved about them in the *Observer* and they still re-form to turn it out on occasion today.)

In 1982 at the Hole in the Ground site (between Castle Terrace and Grindlay Street), so named because that's exactly what it was, a group called Circuit had the bright idea of putting up a tent and turning it into a venue. The Legs were one of the opening acts and sold out their run.

*H*ardee: 'It didn't please us any as we were on a wage. We were all sleeping on the site in tents, so we were a bit scruffy and they had a press conference in the marquee and this commissioner on the door – well, flap – wouldn't let us in as we didn't have ties on. Also there was this feminist troupe there called Monstrous Regiment, I hated them, cos they were doing this play about how awful it was to be in prison but as soon as one of 'em got their handbag nicked they were all for calling the police. Once something happened to one of them their attitude changed – so I was in a mood to get one over on them all.

'At the end of the conference all the acts stood on the bar and gave a small rap on their show. It was all very lovey-dovey. So I got up and said, "As you know, we're the Greatest Show On Legs and are doing a comedy show, but unfortunately I've just read in this newspaper that Glenda Jackson has died. In the spirit of the Fringe, I think we should

Nude cha-cha, with balloons held in strategic positions, had in three minutes secured careers for at least the next three years

observe a minute's silence." They did. Then Martin tugged my leg and passed me up the paper again. "I'm sorry, it's not Glenda Jackson, but Wendy Jackson, an old age pensioner." They went mad.'

Only things got madder when The Legs returned in 1983. Circuit came back not with one tent but four smaller ones and no one had thought about the sound problems this would cause. The running joke of the Festival was 'Go to Circuit, buy one ticket and hear four shows.' It was a situation that put the performers, as much as the audience, on edge.

The running joke of the Festival was 'Go to Circuit, buy one ticket and hear four shows'

Among the stars of the future at Circuit were Emma Thompson, doing a one-woman show of stand-up and sketches (which proved to me at the time that comedy wasn't her forte) and Eric Bogosion. Bogosion, a New Yorker who'd come out of the performance art scene, was an intense performer of sharply written and powerfully acted monologues on the state of America. He was fêted by the London arts community, and his *Voices of America* and *Funhouse* shows were amongst the most distinctive theatrical pieces to grace the country that year. (He has since become an art-house cinema star and now plays top off-Broadway theatres in New York.) He was also somewhat of a prickly character. To put him in the next tent to Malcolm Hardee was to court titanic disaster.

Hardee: 'In our show we used one of those small tractors, used by garden centres and the like, for our entrance. The idea was to build a ramp and jump over some model cars. Now we were in the tent next to Bogosion where he was doing a show called *Funhouse*, which was described in *The Scotsman* as "An anarchistic romp on the American way of life."

'Well, it happened that he started his show three-quarters of the way into ours. And we had specifically put all our noisy stuff into the beginning so it wouldn't disturb anyone else. But just when we got into our quiet bit he had this heavy metal tape on at an extraordinary volume. So after four nights I thought, fuck it, we'll go and see him. Cos I thought it was an anarchistic romp and he'd like that sort of thing. It was only afterwards that we discovered it was a heavy performance art show.

'Luckily you could drive out of our tent up the path and straight into his. So I did. With our audience following behind. There were about four hundred of them, and I was driving the tractor, in the nude as well. I waved to him as I went across the front of his performance space. And at the time he was pretending to play this broom like a rock guitar. He just put his head in his hands as we drove past and out the other side with our audience. Then we went back to our own tent and continued our show, like you do.

'Then there was an awful commotion outside – which I learnt afterwards was Bogosion trying to smash the tractor with his broom. He smashed up his dressing room, then stormed into our show, and I remember his words when he came through. "Hey, you guys, I've lost a

'Luckily you could drive out of our tent up the path and straight into his. So I did. With our audience following behind. There were about four hundred of them, and I was driving the tractor, in the nude as well'

Overleaf: *Rik Mayall (1983)*

lot of money doing this Edinburgh shit." And I remember that well, because his show was all about capitalism and American trauma and all that nonsense. He then saw Martin Soan, who by this time was naked, took a swing at him and missed. He was then bundled out by some Circuit people.'

Robert Llewellyn, who was then a member of the right-on men's comedy troupe The Joeys, was getting ready for his show in the dressing rooms, which were Portakabins:

'We had to pin him down in his dressing room because he was screaming and foaming at the mouth'

*L*lewellyn: 'We were mates with Eric. We actually had to pin him down in his dressing room because he was screaming and foaming at the mouth. And in his raucous and nasal New York accent he was screaming, "They drove a fucking tractor through my fucking show!" He was very upset – he couldn't see the humour of it at all. It's hard to believe it happened now. I went and hid in Emma Thompson's dressing room.'

To avoid having his show axed Hardee was forced to write a letter of apology and pay for all the damage that Bogosion had caused as well as reimburse those who had asked for their money back.

*H*ardee: 'I had to deliver a letter to his flat, which I did, and it was the most sumptuous flat you could imagine in Edinburgh. It stuck in our teeth as we were living in tents again. I gave him the letter and he was horrible. I did try to explain that I thought it was an anarchistic romp, but he wouldn't listen.

'There's an interesting sequel to all this that not many people know about. A year later in June at the Albany Empire [the Fringe theatre in Deptford] they were recording that live chat-show for Channel 4, *Loose Talk*. I came back from the pub one night and I saw a trailer for it featuring an interview with Bogosion. I thought, "Right." I lived 300 yards from the Albany and I had a mate called Mad Mick who had a fork-lift truck hire company which was only 100 yards away. I borrowed a fork-lift off him, drove up to the Albany and slipped a bloke on the side loading door a tenner to open it at the last moment. I tried to drive it in just when he went on stage – but the truck was just six inches too tall.'

Practically every year in Edinburgh, Hardee has come up with one scam or another to promote his show. I'm afraid that any book that tries to look at comedy and the Edinburgh Festival would have to highlight him. He's one of a handful of people that can make those three weeks seem worthwhile. If he wasn't there, the people he torments would probably miss him most – though not, I feel, Eric Bogosion.

Opposite: *Ben Elton (1983)*

Overleaf: *Stand-Up Comedy (1983)*

The Circuit site was also where things started to look up for musical cabaret group Fascinating Aida, a song-comedy outfit who started in the alternative cabaret scene. They were actually far more at home, and indeed about to become very successful, as a theatrically based comedy troupe, but you have to start somewhere and nobody's going to put you into the major London Fringe theatres on spec. You have to prove your worth. By 1983 the London cabaret circuit was big enough to be a spawning ground for all kinds of varied work.

Leader of this particular pack, and now a solo comedy artist, Dillie Keane remembers: 'We got a very late booking there because of a show called *Rock Tartuffe* collapsing.' (This is a story in itself. It was run by a young promoter called Laurence MacKenzie who had started a cabaret gig in London and was hated by everybody on the comedy circuit. When his attempt at theatre failed it cheered up everyone.)

Keane: 'We took it because the space was given to us free. The show was at midnight and it was a sea of mud before you could get to the safety of the tent – we were having to wear wellington boots and carry our high heels.

'We played for three days to six people who were our friends. On the third night a reviewer came from *The Scotsman* and gave us a rave. Then Ian Albery [then head of the Albery Theatre Group, one of the major West End conglomerates] came to see the show, and afterwards came back-stage and savaged us. He told us we looked awful, we needed a director, our make-up was terrible – "You're just a mess – if you're going to do this sort of thing at least get it right.' And he was correct.

'Later on that night I went to a restaurant by taxi – and as I was getting out Nica Burns [an actress, who was to become artistic director of the Donmar Warehouse, the director of the Perrier Award and, now, the deputy artistic director of the Assembly Rooms itself] was getting in. We hadn't talked for years as we'd had an argument. And I said, "Nica, we need a director." She replied, "All right, I'll speak to you later."'

Burns became their director, and though they never got a crack at television, except as subjects of a documentary, they were the first comedy grouping to come out of the eighties able to sustain a West End run. They've now split up, but Dillie Keane was back at the Assembly Rooms in 1990 with her first one-woman show.

Before leaving Circuit, let's just stop in on Jenny Lecoat, who was, along with Helen Lederer and Pauline Melville, one of the few women stand-ups of the early days. In 1983 she decided to put the Edinburgh rumour factory to the test and at the same time have a go at Laurence MacKenzie. (He was never to recover from his experiences at this Festival, and to my knowledge has not been seen since.)

'He told us we looked awful, we needed a director, our make-up was terrible – "You're just a mess – if you're going to do this sort of thing at least get it right" '

Opposite: *Fascinating Aida (1983)*

Lecoat: 'I started a rumour about his *Rock Tartuffe* show purely to see what would happen. I began with the idea he was losing £200 a week. It came back eventually to me that he was losing £12,000.'

Lecoat was also one of the many acts filling in for Simon Fanshawe after Benjamin Zephaniah left him high and dry.

'Benjamin dropped out of Simon's show saying that a friend had died in Jamaica. That was fair enough, but it was a bit fishy when he turned up at the end of the Festival with his own solo show'

Lecoat: 'Benjamin dropped out of Simon's show saying that a friend had died in Jamaica. That was fair enough, but it was a bit fishy when he turned up at the end of the Festival with his own solo show. Like everyone else, I did a set at Simon's show to fill in, then had to run back to my tent to get on stage for my own show. I literally just made it – and ran on to stage out of breath.'

On our way back to the Assembly Rooms our first connection is Bogosion as he was also performing his *Voices of America* piece there, a venue at which he was far happier. It wasn't all down to Hardee. However tough New York might be (though the arts scene is certainly very chi-chi) working in a tent was well beyond Bogosion's capacity. At one point in his show a little boy peeped in through the side door. He went over and slammed it shut, stepped out of character and growled at the audience, 'How can you be expected to work in a place like this?' He missed the point that Edinburgh is a strain on nearly everybody, for only a very few get the chance to play in the better venues. In Peter Brook's seminal collection of lectures on theatre entitled *The Empty Space*, he opens with 'I can take any empty space and call it a bare stage.' In Edinburgh during Festival time his words are taken literally and there is no empty space. It's all filled from the pavement to the grandest theatre with players playing upon it.

In Wilkie House, one of these small spaces turned theatre, Nica Burns was performing that year in a two-hander based on the life of Strindberg. Her leading man was John Dowie, who was also playing the Assembly Rooms in his more usual guise as a comic.

Burns: 'On 27 August it was my birthday and John walked off stage in the middle of the play saying, "I can't go on any more." I apologised to the audience, ran up to him and asked what on earth the matter was. He said, "Don't you ever say that line like that again." By this time I was gibbering with tears. He said, changing his voice totally, "It's your birthday, let's go and buy you a present." Which we did. That was quite an experience – it made me totally wary of ever working with a stand-up in a play.'

Opposite: *Dillie Keane (1983)*

41

Not surprisingly, the Stand-Up Comedy grouping of Elton, Mayall and de la Tour at the Assembly Rooms was the comedy toast of Edinburgh that year. This was not due to the presence of Elton, whose fame as a performer was only going to be secured by compering the second series of Channel 4's *Saturday Live* (as with *Al Fresco* he was first brought in as a writer and then upgraded to full-time performer), but to Rik Mayall.

By this time Mayall was already well known, first brought to the public's notice by his Kevin Turvey character for BBC Scotland's *Kick Up the Eighties* and then, of course, for his invention of Rick in *The Young Ones*. However he wasn't a fully fledged solo performer. He'd only done bits and pieces like his poetry send-up of theatre 'Vanessa', while partner Ade Edmondson was off stage. Indeed on the last night of the original Comedy Store at the end of 1982 Mayall was one of the few acts to get heckled off. Being known on TV made him a legitimate target – times have changed, for now a TV act is regarded with awe.

Being known on TV made him a legitimate target – times have changed, now a TV act is regarded with awe

The third member of Rik Mayall and Ben Elton's team, Andy de la Tour, had been part of the original Alternative Cabaret grouping and one of the central players in the development of the alternative comedy ethos. He fronted a cabaret-style show in the late seventies with political theatre group Belt and Braces, who themselves were going to prove they had a mean comedy talent, successfully turning Dario Fo's *Accidental Death of an Anarchist* into a West End hit. A lefty Fringe group persuading the establishment that a hard-hitting political satire was trendy? With hindsight it is clear that the development of alternative comedy was nowhere near as audacious as it seemed.

' "Can I come?" He really didn't have an act, so he did a bit of Turvey and then had to write some new stuff'

De la Tour: 'Ben and I wanted to go to Edinburgh and we wanted a third person. We were talking about it over lunch and Rik was with us. He said, "Can I come?" He really didn't have an act, so he did a bit of Turvey and then had to write some new stuff.

'We were quite upset at the time when we got there, because people were accusing us of only being there to make money. Originally it was only going to be me and Ben, and at our level we would never have managed to sell out.'

Four years into this new world of stand-up comedy, they were still very uncertain about what could be done professionally.

De la Tour: 'We decided to do a one-and-a-half-hour show without an interval – but none of us had half an hour. Ben and I had twenty-minute sets and Rik only had ten! Ben and I went and did a gig in Putney – Helen Lederer was on the same bill. Both of us did half an hour and we were really frightened.'

Opposite: *Eric Bogosion (1983)*

At the end of 1982 the London listing magazine *City Limits* was persuaded to run a regular weekly cabaret section. The first major interview was with Ben Elton, the tape of which still exists. It's one thing commenting about 1983 with the benefit of hindsight, it's perhaps more illuminating to quote Elton's thoughts at the time:

'I originally tried stand-up to get my writing around. It was obviously terrifying. I was very scared, and have remained scared by gigs ever since. [He started performing in early 1981.] I think I would have calmed down by now if it hadn't been for the Comedy Store. It has done many good things. It's given performance opportunities to a lot of talented people out there – and an enormous number of completely crap people as well – but the bad side is that the gong was abused which has left a lot of comics scarred and I think me most of all. [In the early days an infamous gong was struck to get rid of an act.] Having become compere of the Store for a few months in the summer of eighty-one, I really got a battle instinct with audiences. I don't think that's good and I don't approve of it but I still can't shake the idea of taking on an audience. That was what the Store did to you.

'I'm still scared of audiences even though I'm going to Edinburgh this year, and quite obviously with Rik and Andy it's going to be a very cool show. We're at the Assembly Rooms, a 400-seater and people are going to be paying three notes to get in. It'll be the middle class, it will be no problem. But I know I will still be scared of that audience because I'll be thinking one night my worst nightmare will happen, and suddenly that Comedy Store audience will be out there.

'Like the night we had to call the police. I was compering, and I went off stage and asked for the police to be called. I went back to the microphone and informed the rowdies that the police were on their way and they could either wait or leave now. As Tony Allen said, "If you can't deal with one bunch of thugs, the only real thing you can do is call another bunch of thugs," which I thought was a bit uncharitable at the time – but it was a good joke for the evening!'

De la Tour: 'Ben was always ambiguous about being a stand-up. But that Edinburgh really kicked it off for him. And Rik as well. He'd never felt like a comic before because all he'd done was little sketches. From then on he felt he could do it – and the act he got together for Edinburgh lasted him four years.'

Unlike the other two, it was the beginning of the end for de la Tour. Afterwards he was just back on the circuit and eventually he packed it in to write plays and act again. Now however he goes out every once in a while on a national tour as Mayall's supporting act and these days he's not only got sharper, and, horrors, has new material, he's also far more relaxed on stage. Maybe Andy will one day become one of those classic acts I postulated earlier.

'I really got a battle instinct with audiences. I don't think that's good and I don't approve of it but I still can't shake the idea of taking on an audience'

'If you can't deal with one bunch of thugs, the only real thing you can do is call another bunch of thugs'

Opposite: *Fundation (1983)*

45

There are in fact two watershed years in the eighties for live performance, and both are highlighted by the Festival. In 1986 stand-up became really professional. But in 1983 the Festival show-cased the range of talent available. Part of that talent was going to evolve into what could be described as trendy comedy – the Comic Strip, Alexei Sayle, French and Saunders, Ben Elton, Rik Mayall, John Sessions – later to be joined by Harry Enfield *et al*. But there were also those who were following the path of avowedly more populist entertainment. Lenny Henry was destined to straddle the two.

Hale and Pace's early days were made up of traditional sketches mixed in with songs – alternative comedy's version of *The Two Ronnies*

Hale and Pace were at the Assembly Rooms as part of the Fundation team that produced a practically new show every weekend at The Tramshed, in London's Woolwich. It was the team that had been replaced for a while by the bizarre pairing of Mayall/Edmondson and the early Greatest Show On Legs. Hale and Pace's early days were made up of traditional sketches mixed in with songs. Indeed at the time the Fundation show was described as alternative comedy's version of *The Two Ronnies*.

Norman Pace: 'I think that's pretty fair. We were lucky that we didn't have to trample round like everyone else, but going to Edinburgh was a shock for us. I hated the atmosphere – Gareth did too. There was a great sense of competitiveness and it felt very foreign to me. It left me with a bad taste about the Festival. I didn't feel our show fitted into the Edinburgh Fringe. We've never been a trendy act – and we've resisted the temptation of playing the Playhouse [Edinburgh's biggest venue] during the Festival. We're far happier going and playing it when the Festival's not on.

'The year before we'd played the Café Noir [the room at the top of the Playhouse] and we were booked to do eight shows a week, including Saturday and Sunday lunchtimes. One Sunday there were only four people in the audience – but we decided to do the show anyway. It turned out three were BBC radio producers. One was Alan Nixon who got us a radio series, and these days produces our TV show.'

Hale and Pace's last night of 1983 and their last appearance on the Fringe was also memorable. Norman Pace recalls, 'In the show Gareth used to snap dry spaghetti and then throw it all over the audience. On that last night when he did it a whole bunch of people threw wet spaghetti back. Call me a cynic, but I think the crew had something to do with it.'

Another rowdy story concerns the Stand-Up Comedy crew. Coutts remembers them as being 'nice and quiet. All my staff were in love with them.' But they were joined by Roland Rivron who had been Mayall's backing drummer on *The Young Ones* tour [the birth of Raw Sex]. Andy de la Tour remembers his first meeting with Rivron vividly:

Opposite: John Sessions (1983)

'We had a nice flat near the Assembly Rooms and a lot of people came round. One night Roland Rivron threatened to throw himself out of the window. He wasn't exactly sober and he was sort of challenging the gods to see how far he could lean out. Me and Rik had to grab hold of his legs. I didn't know who he was – he was just a strange friend of Rik's.'

Rivron claims in his own defence, 'It was a good way of finding out who my friends were.' He has only been a passer-by in Edinburgh, otherwise he would be another one about whom the stories would never stop.

1983 was also the very start of John Sessions' career. He was improvising and producing one-man theatrical shows of a very inventive nature well before the current improv comedy boom started. His show that year was entitled *Farting Around*. Coutts says, 'I only remember him for his stage fright. One night he actually had to cancel a show because he was literally sick with fear. It was strange because even then he was such a strong performer.'

1984

The London cabaret circuit began to consolidate in 1984. An early grouping of London-based stand-ups – Nick Revell, Arnold Brown, Paul Merton (then Paul Martin) and Norman Lovett – arrived in Edinburgh calling themselves Brave New Comedy. And another arrived under the generic title 'Off the Kerb Roadshow'. The latter was organised by the first manager/agent/promoter and all-round wide-boy entrepreneur to come from within cabaret. Addison Cresswell is now Julian Clary's manager and indeed mentor; in 1984 he brought up John Hegley and his band the Popticians, Roy Hutchins and Andrew Bailey. A late booking was *The Bad Karma Tour* featuring Nigel Planer and the last gasp of his hippy character Neil, with The Oblivion Boys and Lee Cornes as support. They were part of a national tour organised by Phil McIntyre – a rock promoter who was the first to jump into the new big-time of

Opposite: *Rita Rudner (1984)*

comedy. These days nearly every major comedy tour is handled by his team – he also manages the biggest live act of all, Ben Elton. Alexei Sayle was also doing a couple of gigs at the Playhouse.

The year before had seen enough comics to actually create their own distinct social scene. At this point there were not too many late licences in Edinburgh, and comics as a group function best when looking for that late-night revel. Parties became a regular event. Meanwhile the Assembly Room members bar was the early evening focus point – if you could get in. You were supposed to buy a card for the Festival, but it was always a bit of a game to see how long you could get away without one. Even Coutts had trouble at times: 'There were several occasions when the security staff on the door wouldn't even let me in because I didn't have a pass.' Andy Smart of The Vicious Boys, who were to play the venue regularly, claims, 'We refused to buy a pass. It became a matter of honour to get in. We'd crawl in, smuggle our way in, I even remember juggling past the door guards. Or we just made as much noise as possible – till they had to let us in.'

At the Assembly Rooms the big news was the arrival of Dario Fo and his wife Franca Rame. Fo was to present his one-man show *Mistero Buffo*, a populist and hilarious attempt to explain the history of the Italian commedia dell'arte (the improvised comedy form that was to dominate Europe from the sixteenth to the early eighteenth century). The only trouble was that he gave it in Italian, and his interpreter wasn't exactly *au fait* with the complexities of comic timing. According to Coutts, Fo 'flirted with everybody'. Franca Rame was appearing in the feminist one-woman show which she co-wrote with Fo, *It's All Bed, Board and Church*. Simon Fanshawe witnessed one of her many outbursts.

'The thing about Franca Rame is she's a star – so she behaves like one'

'**F**or some reason I ended up at an Assembly Rooms press conference and there was Franca Rame having a complete scene about something or other. William was sitting there and looking charming about it all. The thing about Franca Rame is she's a star – so she behaves like one. She's screaming and shouting at him then suddenly she decides everything is fine, looks at William, stands up, kisses him on the cheek and says in that purry Italian accent, "Darling, make love to somebody," and leaves. It really made me laugh.'

Revue by this time had finally reached the stage where it was to wither and die. New-wave groups such as The Joeys with their sexual politics slant, or Fascinating Aida, whose antecedents were really several generations before with the likes of Flanders and Swan, brought some life to it; later Kit and the Widow were to tread even more firmly in Flanders and Swan's old musical comedy shoes. But the time of university revue was passed.

Someone who bailed out of revue to find himself eventually landing well and truly on his feet as a stand-up comic was Arthur Smith. He'd been a founding member of the National Revue Company in 1977, and had been a Festival regular ever since with the group. But in 1983 he teamed with fellow member Phil Nice and jumped on the cabaret circuit

Opposite: *Dario Fo (1984)*

in a double act, Fiasco Job Job. He was also destined to become the best live compere in the business: 'Well, there wasn't much competition at the time as nobody liked compering. But I liked it, you didn't need a full set, just a collection of jokes.' He was back at the Assembly Rooms in 1984 with Fiasco Job Job on a double bill with John Dowie. Smith was also one of the party-goers of the year.

Smith: 'It was becoming apparent by eighty-two to eighty-three that sketch shows were old hat. That's the trouble with Footlights, they have to have someone dancing at the beginning of the show. By 1983 we all felt the National Revue Company had run its course. That's when me and Phil formed the double act.

'We'd been going about a year, and this was the first big profile we'd got – not that it was that big a profile, going on at midnight. At first we went on before Dowie, but by the end we were going on last, and coming off stage at about two in the morning. I never got to bed before 7 a.m. that year.

'It was also when I started the Edinburgh Alternative Tours at 3 p.m. and 5 p.m. I used to pick up people as they went along – I got some very bemused customers. I also did one late-night show at about 3 a.m. I offered a guy a quid to be a teapot on a plinth – but he fell down. He was drunk at the time. There was blood on the road – on a yellow line in fact – I distinctly remember that because it was one of those years it didn't rain for the whole Festival. The stain lasted on that yellow line right to the end.'

Fiasco Job Job actually got a Channel 4 series from the Alternative Tours called *Arthur and Phil Go Off*. In fact it was tempting to call this book *Laughing All the Way to Channel 4* as Edinburgh and the Assembly Rooms in particular were going to be fertile ground for independent TV Light Entertainment producers.

Arthur Smith has many stories to tell about John Dowie:

'**D**owie was dead miserable that year. It was well before AIDS and I was being singularly promiscuous. One night I was among the audience watching Dowie, as was the girl of the moment, whose name I probably didn't even know. I was forever stumbling around making introductions like: "This is, um, er. Oh, do it yourselves." Anyway, Dowie started to do a routine about me, about what I was getting up to and started going on about this particular girl: "Smith is now actually picking up girls in chip shops. I wouldn't mind but I can't even get chips in a chip shop." Strangely enough, I never saw her again.

'I offered a guy a quid to be a teapot on a plinth – but he fell down'

Opposite: *Fiasco Job Job (1984)*

'There was also that idea of pissing about on the last night. John went on before us and did all, and I mean *all*, of our material. Every punchline'

'Another time some earnest young comic asked Dowie, as a senior performer, as it were, for his opinion of his act. Dowie destroyed him with, "Give up your crap."

'There was also that idea of pissing about on the last night. John went on before us and did all, and I mean *all*, of our material. Every punchline. Looking back I feel very embarrassed about it – (a) He was pissed (b) He was terrible (c) We were terrible. We tried to busk our way out of it and failed terribly.'

Comedy wasn't a serious occupation in 1984, and Edinburgh acted as a perfect conduit for those who were mad enough to want to do stand-up in the first place – letting off steam after work, as it were, in the early hours of the morning. One of the leading debauchers was original Store performer Oscar McLennan, who was very successful that year with his theatrical performance on the vagaries of living in poverty in London. It involved one sheet and a keep-fit work-out send-up, replete with him wearing leg-warmers and nothing else. Since then he's left comedy and is a serious writer and well-regarded performance artist. He's a sort of latter-day Scottish equivalent of Ireland's Brendan Behan and Wales' Dylan Thomas. For all our sakes it's probably better that he never gets properly discovered. Smith had many a long travail with him:

'I ended up one morning after an all-night drinking session with Oscar in Princes Street Gardens – and I think I was selling cannabis to schoolgirls. Mind you, I was so far gone that I think they actually nicked it off me. I also remember that once Nick Revell, who is by nature very abstemious, was accosted by Oscar and told, "You look terrible, mate." As Nick said at the time, "If Oscar thinks I look terrible, I must be in trouble."'

The following year McLennan was to return with a serious one-man show – he was to get excellent reviews.

Smith himself was to return year in and year out. In 1989 he turned up with a self-penned comedy play two-hander *The Live Bed Show*. It was to prove that he had a lot more to offer than just being an amiable comic. For Arthur, Edinburgh acts as a work stimulant:

'People pick up a lot of ideas there and you come down physically knackered but mentally invigorated. Quite often I conceive things to do for the next year while I'm up there. It also acts as a sort of perfect deadline. You can use it to kill off an old act or produce a new one.

Opposite: *American Comics (1984)*

54

Having said that there's probably somebody who's been doing the same joke up there for the last nine hundred years.'

While the boys were having fun, one of the few female groups in comedy were having a successful but hard time. Dillie Keane of Fascinating Aida recalls:

'We were selling out and getting a lot of flak like "Who are you? You're just middle-class women", from the other performers. There was resentment – but the whole thing was middle class anyway, as was the London cabaret circuit.

'We were also nominated for the Perrier Award – which was hard on Nica [Nica Burns, their director, also happened to be director of the Perrier Award and as such didn't have a vote, so kept leaving the room whenever they were discussed], but these things happen. We were very happy to be nominated – we just said we didn't want the Wangford Band to win.'

Dillie and Hank Wangford were to become best friends, as they say in Country and Western parts, due no doubt to that Edinburgh. Neither of them won the Perrier, it went instead to Californian musical comedy outfit The Brass Band. The latter are a brilliant comedy variety group bringing clowning and classical music together into an act that has true populist appeal. They got together originally as there weren't too many parts for brass instruments in serious music.

Keane: 'Edinburgh helped our career as the only place that used to pay our bills. We were playing places like a church-turned-theatre in Battersea and getting £3.33 to split three ways. As I drove, the others said I should keep the lot.

'I've always found the Assembly Rooms absolute agony. It's so competitive. I remember a comedy bandsman [she won't reveal who, or which band] who would never talk to me. I was approached in the bar by some Radio 4 producer, who wanted me to do something on her show. Then this guy slimed up to me and asked if he could join in. In fact he took over the conversation.

'I also met the poet Adrian Henri there with John Dowie. John tried introduce me – Adrian looked at me and growled a sort of "bleooer" at me, a dismissive condescending noise. John looked startled: "This is Dillie, my friend." He went "bleooer" again – it was nothing recognisable as anything we'd call speech. John said, "She's a member of Fascinating Aida." Henri went, "There you are, you see – I never realised you were famous. I thought you were just another girl hanging around in the bar waiting to be noticed." Which sums up the Assembly Rooms for me.

'I do find the Festival itself aggressively masculine. Female acts are a slow, painful trickle. One year there's a few women, then there's none.'

56

One performer who was destined to play the Assembly Rooms only ever on a very limited number of occasions was maniacal clown Chris Lynam. In 1984 he was to get a one-off show-case in the building as the winner of a buskers' competition.

Lynam: 'The prize was £200 and a month's gigs – it was organised by Alloa Brewery. I was called Chris de Pyss then as me and Chris Langham [part of the original *Not the Nine O'Clock News* team] were forever getting mixed up by bookers. I changed it to Pyss because I thought it fitted in with punk – of course the name failed miserably. The brewery offered to bribe me to change my name, but I wasn't having any. The gigs were cancelled but I still got to do the Assembly one. I used to do a baking sketch and the flour and eggs were likely to go everywhere. They did – it put the nail in me ever playing the place again.'

Not quite – he played there a few years later as the new member of the Greatest Show On Legs. Yes, it's that team again. Lynam was still going to make his mark.

Year after year, the buzz would go round – Where was tonight's party going to be?

The social life of the Festival started to get more than lively this year. The buzz would go round the Assembly bar about midnight: Where was tonight's party going to be? There was always one somewhere – no one needed to put out invitations. Invite one, invite all – everyone was a gatecrasher, you couldn't have kept a soirée secret if you tried. The best example of 1984 was the joint Cliffhanger/Joeys binge. Cliffhanger member Pete McCarthy takes up the story:

'By then *They Came from Somewhere Else* had been on telly, and this gang of punks accosted me outside a pub. I thought, oh dear, this is going to be trouble. But they turned out to be fans of the series. They offered me their New Town flat for a party. I say flat, it was actually burnt out, and I think they were squatting in it.
    'Ian Dury turned up, took all the beer out of the fridge and then left. Things were going very well until the police turned up and confiscated the sound system. In fact they arrested one of the punks and David Jones (a promoter) actually went down and bailed him out.'

The locals of the city must have been heartily sick of the Festival comedy mob by this time – hundreds of people would squeeze into one flat or another and rave to all sorts of hours. A few years later I distinctly recall opening the front door to leave a party at something like 8 a.m., only to discover three Greeks carrying bazoukis (a traditional lute-like instrument), ready to have fun. You can't leave when something like that

Opposite: *Ian Dury (1984)*

happens, and soon everyone was up groovin' away to Greek folk music in the kitchen. They turned out to be the staff of a restaurant The Oblivion Boys frequented, which specialised in late food with drinks till you dropped. Their working day finished at around 6 a.m. – it was Festival time, they wanted to come out and play too.

The Joeys had reached their nadir that year. Besides playing the Ballroom, they were presenting *Edinburgh Inside Out* for Channel 4. Joey, Robert Llewellyn, also recalls someone else who was to carve his way up through the ranks. 'It was very exhausting, doing the show and recording at the same time, but we had a very good researcher, who was also very nice. He was called Jonathan Ross – funny, I don't see much of him these days.'

'We had a very good researcher, who was also very nice. He was called Jonathan Ross'

1985

The big news in town in 1985 was Lenny Henry. He was an easy sell-out in the Assembly's 750-seater Musical Hall but many of the critics were surprised to discover how good a stand-up he was. Henry, who had fallen in with the Comic Strip crowd at the beginning of the eighties, and married Dawn French into the bargain, was making his first steps to become this country's premier stand-up. In the seventies he'd started in the northern clubs, won TV's *New Faces*, and went off playing what's left of the old variety circuit. By the time he became a hit on the kids' show that all the adults loved, *Tiswas*, he still hadn't shaken off the old-fashioned ways. This was highlighted when the show was changed to *OTT* and properly aimed at an after-the-pub adult audience. He invented an African character and put him in a grass skirt, making a stereotyping mistake that was a political affront to the black community. By 1985 he'd become politicised by his association with alternative comedy, and for a while he over-compensated.

'The problem about doing things based on concepts and social comment is that a lot of the time there are no jokes'

Opposite: *Robert Llewellyn (1984)*

Overleaf: *The Joeys (1984)*

Henry: 'I had to back-pedal. In the first three minutes of my first series I talked about periods and all sorts [he breaks into an Elton impression] "My name is LENNY HENRY – GOODNIGHT." I had to find the balance between social acceptance and actually being funny and because I'm from the light variety side I do like jokes, I do like punchlines. The problem about doing things based on concepts and social comment is that a lot of the time there are no jokes. Where's the joke? Hunt the gag.'

By the end of the decade the most talented live comedy performer this country has would finally be recognised as such. He had even overtaken Ben Elton as the comedian with a heart. One can dismiss those that come out with the hackneyed phrase 'It's called alternative comedy because it isn't funny', first because they haven't got the wit to invent a new line for themselves but also, I'd postulate, because without it Henry would never have become as good a comic as he has. And that would have been a sad loss.

Stand-up comedy and new variety acts boomed in 1985. Thanks to the birth of the London cabaret circuit, variety acts now had a place to work again. Indeed original variety performers like paper-tearer Terri Carol also got a new lease of life for a career that was effectively killed by the death of variety proper in the late fifties, early sixties. There were something like fifty shows to choose from across the Fringe.

And there was another major development in the eighties besides the cabaret circuit which was also reflected by the Festival – street entertainment. As with comics, so with buskers; they flocked to Edinburgh from all over the country so that it is now as much a busking festival as anything else. From dawn to dusk The Mound on Princes Street is one great performance area. It is hard to believe that up until 1983 street performance was illegal.

The best act on the busking scene was the musical comedy outfit Pookiesnackenburger – they were brilliant live. Sadly their energies have never been captured properly on record and nor were they able to make the jump to television successfully. They made a Channel 4 series in 1985 with an original concept – extended musical videos with comedy storylines – but it was the live environment they needed.

Arriving from Brighton, they'd been turning up at the Festival since 1979, and they arrived mob-handed, with fellow home-town sea-siders Cliffhanger. In fact in that year they busked together at the Wireworks Playground which was to become an established site.

With their love for the macabre they're a sort of sitcom version of Hitchcock

For Cliffhanger, who started putting comedy plays into pubs in the late seventies, Edinburgh would become a yearly showcase. Their highly original mix of comedy writing, mass culture and their perspicacity (I use that word advisedly as it's the sort they love playing around with) about what makes humans tick has created for them an individual style that no one can possibly copy. With their love for the macabre they're a sort of sitcom version of Hitchcock.

1985 was to be the Pookies' last year; they were splitting at the end of their run at the Assembly Rooms. Coutts remembers, 'They were wonderful. Their last night was so moving – the staff even got together and set up fireworks for them on the stage.' They went out in style – especially on the street. Cliffhanger member Pete McCarthy recalls:

Opposite and overleaf left: *Lenny Henry* (1985)

Overleaf right: *Luke Cresswell as Billy Blurt* (1985)

'In 1984 we made together the most I've ever made in Edinburgh – £500 after one lunchtime street performance. But for 1985 we forgot to apply for our performing licence. We were told by the council that we couldn't perform, and that they'd send the police along to make sure

that we complied. Now these lunchtime shows at the Wireworks had become something of a tradition, it was in the Fringe programme and we turned up and there were hundreds of people there.

'We'd actually discovered another performing space nearby, so I went up to the crowd and told them the police would be turning up soon. When they did, I'd give them a speech about how sorry we all were, and that there wouldn't be any show today, and how they, as a crowd, should show disappointment and disperse. Then when the police had naffed off we'd take them to this other place.

'Which is exactly what happened. A whole crowd acting for us – then they followed me down this alley, and up some steps. Four hundred people – it was like being the Pied Piper. We did this four days running, and the police never suspected a thing. On the fifth day we got our licence issued. Though ten days later we got a letter from the council telling us not to perform in the other place. It's scams like that which make life in Edinburgh worth living.'

'They followed me down this alley, and up some steps. Four hundred people – it was like being the Pied Piper'

At times that year life might not have seemed worth living for McCarthy, who was to be plagued by Oscar McLennan. McLennan had been a feature of alternative comedy since 1979. He'd been discovered while busking by Tony Allen (who in his early days was a regular orator at Speakers' Corner) and became part of the early Alternative Cabaret touring team. A spendthrift, he was always broke, and took great delight in borrowing money off everyone. Anyone who lent him money was totally aware that they'd never see it again. I gave up bothering early on and did a deal where he'd never ask me for money and I'd just buy him drinks (the deal is still functioning more or less – luckily for me he now lives in Dublin). McCarthy however lent him a fiver and foolishly expected it back – he tried winding up McLennan about it every time he saw him. But McLennan was a master at this sort of thing – he'd practically turned it into an art form. For the rest of the Festival, whenever anyone saw McCarthy, they'd go up to him, offer him 10p and say that's from Oscar. McCarthy refused to take them – but if he had, he'd have made a tidy profit. McLennan was incorrigible, but a character as original as his was always going to be encouraged.

He was also going to help put McCarthy in the soup at a certain restaurant. There were very few late licences in the city, and when the Assembly members' bar closed at 1 a.m., a throng would head off to the only late-drinking establishment that could be found that year – a hotel nearby. The hotel cottoned on to this profitable fact early, installed bouncers on the door, then insisted that people bought a meal upstairs before they could go down to the bar below.

McCarthy states, 'I arrived and only wanted a bowl of soup and a glass of wine.'

That's all he had, he joined McLennan, Jeremy Hardy, Kit Hollerbach and myself. Pete paid up and left. We, as a group, were irritated with this hotel to say the least, and after waiting for the bill for fifteen minutes and it still failed to materialise, we left. Well, that's to say McLennan, Hardy and myself left. Kit was swanning around saying goodbye to everybody and asking the waiters, 'Where has my husband got to?' (she and Jeremy are married). Jeremy realised he'd left something behind, worked out in

Opposite: *John Otway (1985)*

Overleaf: *Hull Truck Theatre Company – Bouncers (1985)*

his drunken state it was Kit and headed back, quite bravely I thought, to the place he'd effectively just done a runner from. He was to effect a totally successful rescue.

McCarthy: 'I went off downstairs for some serious drinking. Then on leaving I was stopped by two bouncers who told me I "had to pay this bill". They produced it, I produced my credit card receipt. They were quite heavy about me paying it, or at least knowing who the other lot were.'

He didn't rat on us but did tell them to send the bill to *City Limits* – but then who'd know about a small London magazine in Edinburgh at that time in the morning?

Before leaving McCarthy there's one more story of his worth relating. He shared the same manager as John Deacon of Queen.

McCarthy: 'No one ever recognises John Deacon and we went off to the Comedy Boom together. Then came back to my flat in Stockbridge, which I was sharing with a young Edinburgh architect. My flatmate asked him if he was in a show.

' "No, I'm in a band," he truthfully replied.

' "Oh, that's interesting – I've got a friend who's letting out a church hall if you're interested."

'John didn't say anything, just said he was up here for some fun. When he left I told this guy he'd just told a member of Queen that he could fix up a church-hall gig for him. The poor guy just collapsed into a foetal position.'

'I told this guy he'd just told a member of Queen that he could fix up a church-hall gig for him'

'A big holiday camp for comedians – it's very easy to get gigs in London during August'

The mayhem at the Assembly Rooms continued to the end. Socially there was a party every single night that Festival, from beginning to end. Comedy was finding its feet still – the big stars had all been made at the beginning, the new ones were around but very few saw them as serious contenders. Everyone was pretty well equal and having a good time. Arthur Smith describes it as, 'A big holiday camp for comedians – it's very easy to get gigs in London during August.'

There was also luck and farce going on within the building. Theatrical hit of the year was undoubtedly Teatr Nowy from Poland, whose show was about emigration to America in the early twentieth century. As with many Eastern European companies, they were highly inventive visually, and much of the show was done with life-size mannequins – enabling them to mount quite substantial crowd scenes. The mannequins were basically man-sized stuffed toys which was lucky for one Assembly Rooms technician, who while clambering around in the ceiling of the Music Hall fell on to the stage. From that height he could well have died – instead he fell on to one of the dummies, picked himself up and walked away.

Previous pages: *Brass Band (1985)*

Opposite: *Theatre de Complicite (1986)*

The farce was reserved for Theatre de Complicite, the mime-based company who won the Perrier Award that year for their production *More Bigger Snacks Now*. Their clowning, mime and speech, developed from studying with Le Coq in Paris, was to influence theatre as a whole, and indeed create for them a European audience. The night they won they went upstairs to celebrate in the Assembly Rooms members' bar — only to be stopped by the guardian of the door. They'd walked straight off stage in their gear and weren't carrying their membership cards. The guardian had heard it all before — now some crowd was trying to con him by claiming they'd won an award. These performers would try anything. Mind you, in the main he was right. Complicite went off and celebrated somewhere else.

The previous year's winners, Los Trios Ringbarkus, were back and though their show this year wasn't up to much, they had started a trend. Australian acts felt that the Festival was a good thing for the old profile — from here on in Aussies were to claw their way over. The first of these early comedy migrants was Sue Ingleton. She was like a female version of Barry Humphries — she dressed up and *became* a male character. On stage she was 'Bill the Pregnant Man', as sharp and aggressive as any other Aussie bloke who'd been knocked up. And woe betide anyone coming into her show late, especially as she was in the Edinburgh Suite, a room infamous for the fact that you had to walk across the stage to get in or out of it. Once in, you had to be very brave to leave, even if you were dying to get to the toilet.

My colleague, Carol Sarler, who that year was stringing for the *Guardian* about cabaret, had the temerity to walk into Ingleton's show late — she was wearing her hair quite red that year. 'Oh, look,' hooted Ingleton in her best macho man tones, 'someone's just walked in with a period on her head.'

She was a female version of Barry Humphries. On stage she was 'Bill the Pregnant Man'

1986

Scaffold member, and part of the sixties' Liverpool poet scene, Roger McGough had by 1986 performed in twenty-four consecutive Edinburghs. (He's managed every year since as well.) From the sixties he remembers performing in *Afternoons at the Traverse*:

'There used to be poetry and folk singers; in those days we were the alternative to all the theatricals. The Traverse was very posh then — we were the working-class oiks who were taken on board by the middle class. Larry Adler was around a lot. I do remember going to a great many parties. At one Laurence Harvey was lounging around wearing red slippers with L and H embroidered on each one. We were asked to leave — at least that's what I was told afterwards. I couldn't remember much about it at the time.'

Previous pages: *Los Trios Ringbarkus (1985)*

Opposite: *Julian Clary as The Joan Collins' Fan Club (1985)*

In those days The Traverse was where the actors used to hang out together: 'Once you squeezed in, you couldn't get out again. There was too much of a crush. They were very gregarious and stuck together. They used to bitch a lot – but they were never as funny about it as the comics.'

By 1986 it was the comics who were the social base of the Festival. The Assembly Rooms and its infamous members-only bar room had been the gathering place for the previous few years. But a new venue, the Gilded Balloon, was about to take over. It would run late-night cabarets with a licensed bar till three in the morning. No contest.

McGough, reflecting the changes at the Festival, was performing with comedian Pete McCarthy in 1986. He was even putting one-liners into his act: 'My favourite time at the Festival was watching the Castle being built.' For McCarthy this was what the Festival was about: 'Roger had come to see Cliffhanger a few years earlier. Here was a hero of mine, watching me. Then we met and got on.' McGough was also to write for dance-theatre troupe The Kosh through meeting them at the Festival. They too could be found socialising with the comics.

Alternative comedy hasn't boomed simply because it is new, it has had to create its own market. For years the comedy scene was very small and for the majority of the acts very badly paid. Only a few of the originals went on to TV glory early, many of them having done their performance time in the seventies as part of Fringe theatre. What really changed things was Thatcher. It wasn't that alternative comedy got going at the tail-end of punk, and so wasn't it lovely to be having a go at the Right? It was because the Right was taking away subsidy from the arts. Soon the energies of creative performers were expended chasing far too small grants – something had to give. Stand-up had arrived. All you needed was yourself, and, if you were lucky, a microphone. It was cheap and it was certainly cheerful. Audiences could spend a couple of quid, have a drink, a smoke and feel they were getting away from the hackneyed TV variety diet. Ironically alternative cabaret fitted right into the Thatcherite ethos – you really could get on a bike, then get on a stage and run your own business. Innumerable stand-ups, in fact, used the Enterprise Allowance Scheme to get going. They put up £1000 and then the State paid £50 a week for a year plus housing benefit, no questions asked. Well, if comedy cannot be ironic, what can?

Someone who certainly didn't need to be performing at the Festival that year was Rory Bremner. He already had his own telly series, *Now Something Else* screened in March 1986, and had become a star inordinately quickly.

Bremner: 'By the end of eighty-seven I began to realise that the Assembly Rooms was a better slot for the likes of Jeremy Hardy and Julian Clary – so I ducked out, specifically because I thought it should be a platform for Fringe comedians, not TV stars. Mind you, having said that, I am intending to go back there for 1990 to work in a new show.'

As a local boy Bremner has more rights than most to be there.

Alternative cabaret fitted right into the Thatcherite ethos – you really could get on a bike, then get on a stage and run your own business

Opposite: *Eric Bogosion (1985)*

Overleaf left: *Roger McGough (1986)*

Overleaf right: *Roger McGough and Pete McCarthy (1986)*

81

'I was born in Edinburgh, and used to watch all the university revues in the late seventies. It made me want to do what I do now. I still have the old programmes. I used to watch people like Rory McGrath. These days he jokingly suggests we should do a show called *The Two Rorys*, where he stands up and takes the piss out of me.

'At first I used to work up there during the Festival. I was a porter in a hotel and I remember rigging a fruit machine so Annie Lennox could win more money.'

Bremner got his chance to perform by going to London University, and then coming back up to Edinburgh with them in the university's revue (a bit more of the old comedy irony).

'It was called *The Importance of Varnish*. My happiest times were walking along Princes Street at 11 p.m. one evening and thinking that something was happening all over the city at that moment. That was the real bug.

'In Edinburgh, even if you're in a medical revue, as long as you're in a show you're on the same level as anyone else. The humblest performer feels as much a part of the Festival as the rest. That's what's good about it – and still is. But now it's very much a talent show up there and it's a great pity that's happened. Edinburgh has become very much like a large box of chocolates for TV and radio producers.'

Bremner's comedy line on the Festival was, and still is, 'The quietest time is when you're doing your show.' He'd gone from being just a fan five years previously to being that year's hot young thing.

'It was extremely exciting. Looking back there's something perverse about extensive coverage of those who are already discovered but I wasn't aware of that at the time.' It was so exciting, in fact, that Now Something Else did happen: 'It was during that run I got engaged to my wife, Susan. Best gig I did that night.'

Bremner draws attention to another feature of 1986 that marks how the Festival was changing: 'Pola Jones/Phil McIntyre took me up there. They were big managements and they put up big professional posters with professional teams.' (Bremner was depicted in a naughty near-nude pose.) It was the beginning of the poster wars. London comics and managers thought that since they had taken over the Festival, they could take over the wallspace too. One wall got postered so heavily it actually collapsed.

While the professional teams postered more to oblige certain egos than for the general public's benefit, one particular comic suffered quite badly. Paul Merton was amiably splashing glue on a wall ready to add his face to the comic montage when he was set upon and beaten up by a crew of Scottish lads. No one knows if they were local poster boys defending their space, drunks, or early Greens protesting about deforestation.

Jack the Lad promoter Addison Cresswell describes an occasion two

'In Edinburgh, even if you're in a medical revue, as long as you're in a show you're on the same level as anyone else'

Opposite and overleaf left: *Rory Bremner (1986)*

Overleaf right: *Steve Steen of Sweeny and Steen (1986)*

84

'These two big Glaswegians who were putting up posters pointed out that it would be a shame if a nice middle-class boy like me should come to any harm. I could see their point'

years later when he was taken aside in the bar of the Assembly Rooms. 'These two big Glaswegians, who were putting up the posters for a big management, pointed out that it would be a shame if a nice middle-class boy like me should come to any harm. I could see their point. We speedily came to an agreement whereby they could have the top half of walls and we could have the bottom. It worked out well.' The poor independent comic was being squeezed out.

In 1989 postering would become really farcical. Archaos, the completely wonderful and completely mad French Circus troupe, hit town and plastered their posters all over a police box. It was a pretty audacious thing to do – especially as there was a policeman inside at the time!

Alongside Bremner at the Assembly Rooms in 1986 was Dave Baddiel. Now a successful radio comic (and who knows how close telly fame may be for him), he was then a member of the Cambridge Footlights. Footlights had had an easy ride for years, but now stand-up had well and truly arrived they found themselves faced with serious competition.

*B*addiel: 'We were the first Footlights revue to happen in the Assembly Rooms. We organised it and thought it was brilliant. But it quite quickly became clear it was a mistake. Footlights are a critical target in Edinburgh – and we highlighted our target. We always sold out but *The Scotsman*'s critic trashed the show.'

*F*our years on and Baddiel can still quote the review's punchline. (When a comic starts remembering a critic's material you know it has really hurt.) Owen Dudley Edwards had written: 'On this illumination from the Footlights the Cam is an open sewer.'

'*T*hat had a big effect. We didn't get away with the show after that. On the first night it went down a storm – afterwards the audiences were still turning up, but they were expecting it to be shit. It wasn't a great experience. I was also having disagreements with other members of the cast. I hated the president of the Footlights at the time, even though I'd written with him for three years. Basically, he was a complete wanker.'

*T*here is a famed animosity to Oxbridge from the new breed of comics – how did he fare?

Opposite: *Cambridge Footlights (1986)*

Overleaf left and right: *Ben Keaton (1986)*

'I remember meeting Jeremy Hardy in the toilets and he asked, "Do you come out at the start of your show with a clipboard?"'

'It was noticeable. We were sharing a dressing room with Jenny Lecoat and Rory Bremner. He was friendly. She was always cold and distant – and she sent someone over to tell us to stop singing.

'I was doing stand-up in that show. I really admired all the alternative comics. I remember meeting Jeremy Hardy in the toilets and he asked, "Do you come out at the start of your show with a clipboard?"

'My experience with the Footlights didn't help my career. Once you get accepted into the comedy club it's a great laugh but in Footlights you were marked like a leper, it was awful.'

In 1988 the Oxford Revue were to walk into the lions' den without knowing it. They accepted a booking to perform at the Gilded Balloon's late cabaret show *Late 'n' Live*. It was a set-up. Every comic in town showed up – this was, after all, the Comedy Store moved north for August. It was harmless, or maybe harmful, sport for them but the Oxford group didn't know what had hit them. In Edinburgh it's normal to go and play lots of late-night gigs to advertise your show. You don't expect an audience that spends its life dealing with heckling to do the heckling. The poor things didn't even realise that to handle a crowd you use the microphone provided. Patrick Marber, who started as part of the Oxford Revue, was sitting at the back with his coat over his head squawking, 'It's my roots. It's my roots.'

Before we leave 1986 we should go back to that Hole in the Ground. This time the last of the original hippy groups, Elephant Fayre (who run the highly successful summer festival) had taken it over and erected their large tent. They didn't produce anything untoward – indeed it was a vast improvement on the old Circuit days.

Time Out, on the other hand, should have been given an award for bravery. They put on a nightly talk-show which was certainly not a critical success, and it didn't really take off with audiences. One of the many japes, or let's be honest cock-ups, was down to John Dowie again. Arthur Smith and Muriel Gray were the hosts and Smith had just interviewed his old mucker Dowie. Muriel then went on to talk to the next guest, Stephen Fry. Dowie, already somewhat the worse for wear, suddenly stumbled back on stage to inform the startled audience loudly: 'I've just done some amyl nitrate – it's wonderful.'

Opposite: *Jenny Lecoat (1986)*

Overleaf: *Denise Black and the Kray Sisters (1986)*

92

1987

In 1986 a buzz went round the Festival that there was a great new Scottish comic performing at the Café Royal at 2 a.m. I distinctly remember plodding round there time and again to try and catch him, but he'd either gone or wasn't going to be on for hours yet, and at that time of the morning during the Festival you're either very tired, or very drunk – usually both. I never did get to see him. His name was Bing Hitler; now better known as Craig Ferguson.

*F*erguson: 'That was the start of my career. I got a couple of good reviews. I slept three times a week on Waverly Station – broke, on the dole and living in Glasgow at the time. The last train was at 12.30 a.m. and some of the audience were usually stuck at the station as well. It was disgusting, there was nothing glamorous about it – I'd wake up in the morning with a stinking hangover. It's not a great way to start a showbiz career. I remember being in the queue for a hamburger at the station and this guy in front of me turned round and told me he'd seen the show and how great it must be to be in showbiz. He was in the queue with me! Yer, it's really glamorous, mate.

'I remember thinking that year that the big place to do would be the Assembly Rooms – and then thinking what a toilet it was. I wouldn't like to be starting as a stand-up now – the flocks of cabaret boys from London hadn't appeared then. Now there are too many.'

'I remember thinking that year that the big place to do would be the Assembly Rooms – and then thinking what a toilet it was'

*F*erguson's views on the London cabaret scene tend to be dismissive but then he has due cause. Though he did make it to the Assembly Rooms, partnering Harry Enfield, whose act had just taken off on *Saturday Live*, 1987 was to be a bad year for him. Fellow Glaswegian comic Gerry Sadowitz was in the small Wildman Room, Ferguson was in the larger Ballroom. Sadowitz wrote about himself in his Fringe programme entry: 'Too offensive for telly, he's had his act ripped off by Bing Hitler and his material stolen for television and radio.'

*F*erguson: 'I sued Sadowitz for libel – now with hindsight I wouldn't do it. It is the greatest affront to a stand-up to be accused of nicking material – I know everyone says he's mad, but you can't let someone get away with something like that. I wouldn't do it now because it gave him publicity and gave me adverse publicity.

'The whole Festival was ruined for me by that libel action – it was just awful, the worst time of my professional career. You think everyone in the audience believes you're a kleptomaniac.

Previous pages: *Hank Wangford Band (1986)*

Opposite: *Harry Enfield as Stavros (1987)*

Overleaf: *Craig Ferguson as Bing Hitler (1987)*

'When stand-ups get together they're a loathsome breed'

'The London cabaret circuit acted like animals – they backed Sadowitz as one. It changed my attitude to it. That's why I wouldn't have anything to do with it. When stand-ups get together they're a loathsome breed. Only Addison Cresswell and Roland Muldoon [director of Hackney Empire] didn't take sides. The hypocrisy is that when you get on, they think you'll forget but it broke my heart more than any woman ever has. It still makes me angry and I still don't talk to Gerry Sadowitz.

'He settled out of court – I sued the Edinburgh Fringe Programme and any monies he lost were charged by them. Now I can't go to see his show though I'd like to. If he hadn't done it he might have been a friend. There aren't exactly many Glaswegian comics around.'

Ferguson may have had a bad time, but the Festival gave him a profile that he would have had to struggle to attain any other way in 1987. In fact he's the only comic of recent times who has been able to develop ignoring London. In 1989 Ferguson did a one-nighter at the Playhouse during the Festival and, although he didn't fill it, with over 2000 people he did better that night than the Chinese opera which was part of the official programme. In 1990 Ferguson was signed up by Granada for his own TV series.

In contrast Gerry Sadowitz had to leave Glasgow and come to London to get recognition. A good magician and an hilarious comic, it is his nihilism which gets in the way of him becoming a big act. But then maybe that's where the power of his performance lies. At times he has been referred to as the Bernard Manning of the new-wave, but it's equally true that he is an extremely talented live performer. Like Ferguson he was to find it a hard slog to get going.

Sadowitz: 'I used to cheat to get ten minutes on stage supporting a rock band. I would go into a pub where a band was on, go up to the band and say I was a regular there and that I usually did ten minutes of comedy. When they agreed I had to go up to the pub manager and pretend I was the band's support. I sometimes got a drink and a bit of food out of it but it was the live experience I needed.'

Sadowitz was also a regular street act – a talent I saw him employ at London's Comedy Store one night. The audience these days is reasonably boisterous but in the mid-eighties it could be positively daunting. Sadowitz was on stage when his mike died. He continued to do his set and held the packed audience, hecklers and all, in what is a terrible acoustic space. In 1986 he played the Royal Scots Club, which was 'doubly useful as it gave me the chance to play to Scottish audiences and it gave me a lot of publicity'.

Asked about the 1987 affair with Ferguson Sadowitz is unmoved: 'I don't regret any of that – except I lost a lot of money that year.'

Opposite: *Gerry Sadowitz (1988)*

Comedy is a small, enclosed world at the best of times; during the Festival it's practically hermetic. Every year it seems like the last year hasn't happened at all; one Festival blends into another, the people are basically the same, and you could practically start your first conversation where you left it the year before. It's not surprising that when you put such a large quantity of performers' egos into such a small space the occasional explosion occurs. The closer they are pushed together, the more excited they get – and then look out.

Sadowitz claims he gets a bad press – and these days I tend to sympathise with him. Once you've set yourself up as a target, the papers aren't going to let you go.

Sadowitz: 'It's a very Scottish thing to slag off their own comics. Harry Lauder didn't get any attention, went off to the States and became a star. Then the Scots referred to him as "Our Harry Lauder".

'When I started out I was trying to go for left-wing and right-wing targets but, for instance, in the gag that everyone has a go at they leave out the punchline: "Nelson Mandela – what a cunt. Terry Waite, a bastard. You lend someone a fiver then you don't see them again." People just quote the first line.'

Someone else who had a disastrous 1987 was Paul Merton, a surreal comic who'd been around since the early eighties. This was to be his first crack at Edinburgh with a one-man show. He was at that point in his career where things were really about to break for him but unfortunately he was a little out of condition and while joining in with other comedians for a kick about in the park he broke his leg. 'I wouldn't mind if I'd been tackled – but I tripped over my trousers.' This was right at the start of the Festival, a calamity enough, but things got worse. 'I developed a blood clot that nearly killed me, then caught Hepatitis A from the hospital food.' The comedy community closed ranks, didn't joke about it once they realised the bad way he was in, and rallied to keep his show going. Till the end of the Festival all the acts played it and, as many were headliners, word got round to audiences, so Merton made a healthy profit from his hospital bed. He was to come back the following year, play the Assembly Rooms and call the gig appropriately *Paul Merton's Break-a-Leg Show*. He is now one of the stars of *Whose Line Is It Anyway?* and co-writes *Sticky Moments* with Julian Clary.

For the stand-ups the annual Perrier Award for best comedy show on the Fringe was becoming increasingly important. The year before one of their number, Roy Hutchins, just missed out to a more theatrically based, scripted piece by actor Ben Keaton called *Memoirs of an Irish Taxidermist*. (Incidentally, both Hutchins and Keaton were mime-trained.) This year all five nominations went to stand-ups and only one was supported by a musical act.

Character comic John Sparkes, who by now had joined BBC Scotland's *Naked Video* team, was one of the nominees, directed by Alan Nixon, a radio producer at the time. Sparkes is now a member of Channel 4's *Absolutely* team and, yes, his producer is Nixon.

Opposite: *Gerry Sadowitz (1988)*

Overleaf left: *Paul Merton (1988)*

Overleaf right: *Arnold Brown (1988)*

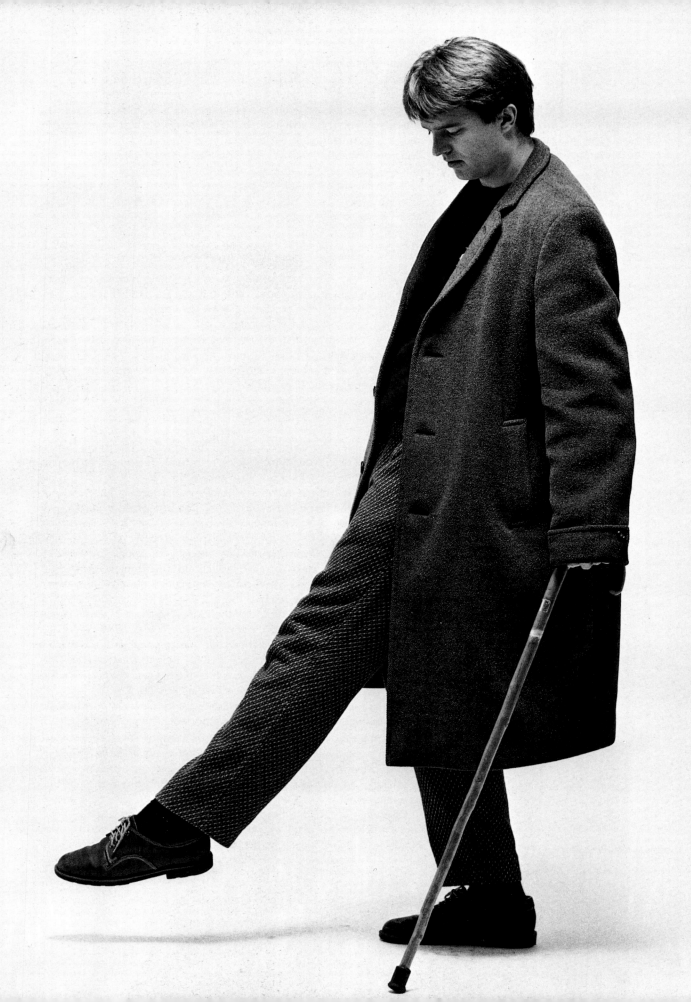

Sparkes: 'It was my first solo show – and going from thirty minutes to an hour is a daunting prospect. The first few shows I found difficult, then I began to enjoy myself, then I was nominated for the Perrier. That actually spoilt it. I started worrying about judges and whether I'd win it. Before it hadn't bothered me, but once I was nominated I wanted to win.

'In a sense it produces an unpleasant competitive quality. I almost resented being chosen. When I didn't win I got disappointed but if I hadn't been nominated, I wouldn't have been.'

Also shortlisted with Sparkes were Simon Fanshawe, Nick Revell, Jeremy Hardy and Brown Blues (Arnold Brown and musical act Barb Jungr and Michael Parker) – all comics who knew each other well and had played the same gigs together for years. Brown Blues was to win, and in some ways the comics themselves were relieved. Everybody was happy for Arnold. He was one of the true originals, there on the opening night of the Comedy Store – an accountant whose attempt at stand-up was filmed by *Nationwide*. From now on cabaret, and especially stand-up, was to dominate totally the award.

To the outside world an award like Perrier may not seem very important but it does help careers, generates a lot of favourable publicity, and puts the winner into the limelight for TV producers. In the old days they scouted Oxbridge revues for talent. Now they can let a panel of judges go out and scour the Festival for them. After all, if any of the student revues are any good they are in with a chance – in 1981 the Footlights won it with that dream cast. But, in the false world of stand-ups, striving to capture the attention of audiences against a sea of fellow sharp-arsed chatterers, tension does build.

Perhaps this tension was also due to the performers getting bored. There are always eager new people, but for the majority in 1987 it was yet another year. By now they were sussed enough to be in the better digs, the better venues, but it was getting a bit like having to stay at a party right to the bitter end because you couldn't get a cab home.

Lecoat: 'I first started to get a bit jaded with it that year. Having the same conversations with the same people. Also, I realised that getting a show together for Edinburgh was not a viable project – it had to be one that you really wanted to develop, and tour with afterwards.'

'The desperation to have a good time and enjoy yourself so much you become ill. It's difficult to avoid drinking'

Opposite: *Jenny Lecoat and the Diamantes (1987)*

Sparkes: 'It's the sheer amount of people there, and the carousing – the desperation to have a good time and enjoy yourself so much you become ill. It's difficult to avoid drinking – the temptation is far too great. You do a show, you want a drink. You meet people you know and like – before you know it it's three in the morning and you're dead.

'It's a great relief to come home. These days when I'm up there I have more of a mind to go to the Botanical Gardens during the day – it's relaxing and the squirrels are friendly.'

Though stand-up does for the moment dominate the Fringe, there is still another strand of theatrical comedy present. The National Theatre of Brent have in the eighties created their own distinct style of epics – using two people – without much contact with the wider new-wave comedy fraternity. Founder Patrick Barlow tells how he plotted his own course.

'It was 1979 and I was performing at the National as well as doing a street show at Brent Park – the most bizarre job of my life. I got the idea to do *The Charge of the Light Brigade* on my own. I put the National and Brent together because I thought it was a great pretentious title for pretentious men doing an epic on *The Charge*.'

He put the show together for the Old Red Lion in Islington, a small Fringe pub venue in London, and to his surprise 'The arts council came to it and offered us money to do a new show. Such a thing was unheard of.' The likelihood of this happening to anyone nowadays is really less than zero. Their new production was *Zulu* and they took it to Edinburgh in 1981. They played The Wildcat and the reaction to that 'put us on the map'.

'Actually on the third night, half-way through the show, a black member of the audience got up and did the Amandla power chant. It wasn't aggressive – nor a piss take. Then he sat down. Everyone presumed it was part of the show but we were just frozen on stage.

'I never then, nor indeed now, feel part of anything alternative. I never watched shows like *The Young Ones*. But as a result of doing The National Theatre of Brent I know a lot of alternative comedians. We did the Amnesty Show and I began to see links. It was organised by John Cleese and there were the Pythons, *Not the Nine O'Clock News*, *The Young Ones* and Peter Cook and Dudley Moore. I don't know where we fitted in but I felt part of something then. Backstage at the show everyone was watching the monitors. I'm sure the old comics must have been like that. There's a great sense of learning and getting it right.

'We all look back longingly at that other age. Ade Edmondson's got Tommy Cooper's trunk. What's happening now is completely different – you can't compare Dickie Henderson to, say, Rik Mayall. It was great to see them all watching each other's acts and wishing each other well – Ben Elton commenting "Now that's comedy" all the time.

'The great thing about Edinburgh is everyone watching everyone else's shows. Ruby Wax came up to us and asked, "Shit, how did you do that? We've been trying to write like that for ages." It wasn't stroppy – she just wanted to know. People don't slag each other off – that I think is nice.'

'Ruby Wax came up to us and asked, "Shit, how did you do that? We've been trying to write like that for ages"'

Opposite: *National Theatre of Brent* (1985); and overleaf left: (1983)
Overleaf right: *The Vicious Boys* (1986)

Hmm. If he thinks the comics don't slag each other off, then you can see how Edinburgh changes depending on your perspective. Bitches United don't play a grudge derby with Slaggers Town every day but it does sometimes feel that way. The whole thing is undoubtedly made worse by the fact that performers are usually trying to make it at the Festival – once you're successful the pressure's off.

Still people do learn from each other and as you'd expect with performers they sometimes do it in public. Andy Smart, half of the slapstick duo The Vicious Boys, describes one occasion.

'It's a great place to meet people from other countries. There were these three Spanish mime artists who had a routine where they did a fake kick in the balls. They couldn't speak English, we couldn't speak Spanish. They came to see our show in the Assembly Rooms and tried to say they liked it. We asked them a favour – would they teach us to kick each other in the balls? This was all done by mime of course.

'We were doing this in the Assembly Rooms foyer, which was packed as usual with crowds queueing for shows. We moved the crowd back to give us a space and in the end there were five people kicking each other in the bollocks. The crowd didn't know we were mucking about and they totally freaked out.'

1988

Things had been getting a trifle cosy in Edinburgh but luckily two hundred years before 1988 Australia had been founded. To celebrate the bicentenary a whole boatload (well, not everyone likes to fly) of Aussie comics came a visiting under the reasonably witty title of 'Oznost'. It was a pretty mixed pouchful and some 'rooed' (sorry) the day they decided to come. But there was one performer who really did bring the spirit of adventure with him. In fact he epitomised what the Fringe should be – mad, bad and quite fun to know. His name was Rod Quantock and his audience, the performers, and the stage he set for them was the City of Edinburgh. It was the one empty space that no one had thought of using.

Quantock had a bus, and in that bus he'd get forty people to put on Groucho Marx masks and read a song sheet. After that the rest of the trip would take in whatever took his fancy – one involved everyone bending down and sneaking past the security guard at the main post office sorting centre. What could the guard do? Say, 'Halt, who goes there – friend or foe?' to a bunch of people wearing Groucho masks and singing?

Quantock became an infamous character. On his first night out he visited a massage parlour which was not used to such rough treatment.

He epitomised what the Fringe should be – mad, bad and quite fun to know

Opposite and overleaf: Rod Quantock (1988)

114

Coutts: 'The woman in charge wasn't at all happy. She got on to the police. Quantock was miked up because a TV crew were shooting him and the police caught up with him in the street. He inveigled himself into someone's flat and took the police with him because they wanted a quiet word. They cautioned him and it was broadcast.

'I went on a tour with him in Australia. One guy who was drunk got on board because he thought it was the bus to Gringuid. He woke up fifteen minutes later and he was surrounded by all these people wearing Groucho masks singing away merrily. Later when we got into someone's house he phoned up his wife and tried to explain what was going on. I don't think she believed him.'

And on the subject of capers, as usual Malcolm Hardee was in town. We all know about the three R's but Hardee comes from the school of the three Ir's – irreclaimable, irredeemable and irrepressible. Clown Chris Lynam is from the same school. When the two of them joined forces in a re-formed Greatest Show On Legs it was a case of 'Nitro meet Glycerine . . . What happened?'

That year they were performing at the Comedy Boom – a small cellar under a pub opposite the Playhouse. Chris Lynam had been working a completely mad routine for the last year or so. He'd stick – and there's no delicate way of describing this – a firework up his backside and light it. One evening The Legs got their entire audience out on the street. Lynam appeared starkers on the pub steps, bent over and Hardee inserted a banger. He lit it and stood well back. Maybe one should condemn this sort of action, but when you see it for the first time – especially with passers-by stopping and ogling – I defy you not to have hysterics.

They had done it outside that evening as the landlord had 'freaked' the night before when they did it inside. According to Lynam the following night 'there were five plainclothes police standing at the back – so we decided against it, though Malcolm wanted me to so we'd get arrested. He loves a good publicity stunt.' Malcolm got his wish for publicity in a big way a few days later . . .

Julian Clary was playing the Supper Rooms of the Assembly complex, but in the middle of his run had to go to London and do some TV work. The Legs were offered the space.

Hardee: 'By a complete coincidence I'm a friend of the Chief Fire Officer of Edinburgh, Maurice Gibb. I met him back in eighty-one and he comes to all our shows. We got the banger-up-the-bum routine passed by the fire officer and we did the first night no problem. The second night all hell broke loose. The fire alarm went off and the whole building had to be evacuated. Me and Chris Lynam had to leave naked as it was just after the balloon dance.

'We were standing at the door of the Assembly Rooms in the nude, surrounded by thousands of people. Now who should be the first fireman to jump out of the engine but Maurice Gibb. He summed the situation up very quickly, "Oh, I thought so." And he just told all of his men to go back.'

Lynam appeared starkers on the pub steps, bent over and Hardee inserted a banger. He lit it and stood well back

Opposite: *Malcolm Hardee (1988)*

119

The next night they did the stunt outside, on top of Malcolm's car. 'That was much more dangerous – only a few feet from a petrol tank.'

'I'm more maniacal than most, but it's controlled mania'

Lynam: 'Coutts won't talk to me – he won't ever give me a job. Sure, I'm more maniacal than most, but it's controlled mania. The fire brigade had told them to turn off the fire detector for our show.'

It wasn't going to be Lynam's year at all. Doing the can-can as part of a Legs' set at the late-night Gilded Balloon cabaret gig, he did the splits and wrenched his hamstrings. 'I couldn't get up. But being the good soldier I am, I sung from that position till the ambulance picked me up.'

Hardee was on a roll that year. He thought up the Snakebite Award for the worst comedy show at the Festival. This sent up the Perrier nicely and gave him and his mates an excuse to see shows for free. Most importantly, it gave Hardee publicity. Anyone who wanted to could become a judge – he printed cards and off they went. Hardee managed to get into the official Festival's opera at the Playhouse with one. By 1989 it had become an institution. He was also to pull off the best scam he's managed yet. As with such things it was deliciously simple, and it's well worth waiting a chapter for.

The Perrier itself was won by another stand-up – though, in fairness, the shortlist was wide ranging. There were anarchic sketch team The Wow Show, Australian musical comedy trio The Doug Anthony Allstars (incidentally the biggest Australian success – and they were the only ones who had to pay their own way over), *Mammon*, a comedy play from Robert Llewellyn, and Roy Hutchins with tales of his childhood *Space-hoppers, Clackers and Really Big Fish*. Hutchins was in many ways the hit of the year, not for his comedy but for his solo performance of Heathcote Williams' epic environmental poem *Whale Nation*. He was directed by John Dowie.

The winner was Jeremy Hardy – undoubtedly the best political comic to develop out of cabaret since Ben Elton. Like Elton, he also set off on the path of humour writer and then turned to stand-up. He wasn't overjoyed to win the award – the first thing he said was 'I think Roy Hutchins should have won it.' He went on in his interview with *The Times*:

'I loved his show. It had far more consequence than mine – a great depth, passion and humanity that my show doesn't have. I'd like the definition of comedy and cabaret to be more flexible. I'm rather sad that it has come to mean half a dozen comedians doing their bit on a bill somewhere. It is because stand-up is becoming so commercialised that there is less room for imagination and variation.

'I'm not putting down what I do. I make people laugh and I think I'm good at that, but in the long run I want to do more; I try to do that now – to make people think. I just think the pressure is there to behave yourself, and be neutral and bland. I hope I haven't done that – I hope there is passion and commitment in what I do.

Opposite: *Roy Hutchins (1988)*

Overleaf left and right: *Jeremy Hardy (1988)*

120

It wasn't all bad. He finished: 'My car's packed up so the money will be handy.'

The main difference between Hardy and Ben Elton is one of attitude. From the beginning Elton was a hard worker, a mover and a groover. He felt passionately about what he was saying on stage, but he was a diplomat. He played the game with all the commitment of the young executive who wants to be managing director – one day he will be. Hardy has something of an abrasive reputation – off stage, as well as on – he takes no prisoners.

*H*ardy: 'It's interesting that all the Oxbridge bastards are stand-ups these days. Stand-up is your passport to TV – not sketches.

'It's nice to feel part of a big festival – once a year you bump into Roger McGough and say how are you. It's also good to go up there – the London cabaret scene is a cushy life, the Scots are dour bastards. You have to work hard. The Scots are wary of being hectored, which isn't particularly good for someone like me who likes hectoring, and they are more politicised, they demand a joke for their money.

'The reason Edinburgh is called the Athens of the North is because it's full of English people throwing up everywhere.

'Your material grows because you're in your own little world for three weeks. I find every year, within the first week, my set's grown by twenty minutes.'

*O*ne story from Edinburgh quickly made it into his set. Here's what actually happened.

'In eighty-seven, me, Kit (Hollerbach), Mark Steel and Tony Hawkes were sharing a flat and there was a mistake about the date we were supposed to leave. We were partying away on the last night of the Festival and at 9 a.m. the next morning three of us were asleep. Tony Hawkes was walking towards the lavatory with an early morning stonker. There was a ring on the door and it was this Dr McQuillan, whose flat it was, asking us to get out. Kit started screaming at him, and the rest of us tried to cover up all the damage we'd done. Then he started telling us all about his guns. "I've had a lot of trouble with my licence since all of this Hungerford nonsense." That made up our minds that we should leave.'

*R*obert Llewellyn first came to Edinburgh in 1982 as part of The Joeys. 'The woman who brought us up was Jeanette Winterson, now the author of *Oranges are not the Only Fruit* and *Sexing the Cherry*. We didn't know what we were doing – we just sort of stuck up a couple of posters and hoped people would turn up. I wasn't sleeping or eating – except doughnuts for some reason. I ended up very ill.' Six years on, he was

'The reason Edinburgh is called the Athens of the North is because it's full of English people throwing up everywhere'

Opposite: *Panic Brothers (1988)*

playing in the relative safety of the Assembly Rooms – 'relative' because although it gives you a good profile, a press officer and at least some audience, it's a risky proposition. You have to do a high percentage of business before you make any money at all – and if you fail, you're going to be owing a lot. Llewellyn was especially bold – he brought a comedy play with a sort of cabaret feel, about the construction of a macho robot. It was original – but these days originality isn't what you take as a financial bet.

'It was all done on the never-never. If it hadn't worked – I would have been in trouble. We all travelled up in one car and I felt too old to be doing it – oh no, not again! Three of us were in a VW Golf, with all the equipment, bedding and clothes. We had two punctures on the way up and three on the way down! Luckily I was in the AA.

'It started off with small audiences, but it took off and saved my bacon. It was very much a turn round for me, I've been busy ever since. Talking about it, I feel like going back. I also fell in love with another performer, Judy Pascoe. The rest of the Festival is a blissful blur.'

The previous year's Perrier-winner Arnold Brown was also playing the venue, in a bill with Simon Fanshawe and Scots poet Liz Lochead. 'When I first came up in eighty-three it was casual. You didn't think what you were doing was momentous. Now there's a TV producer round every corner – every performance has to be high energy. By eighty-nine I was very serious about it, I never socialised. I just went to a café in the afternoons and worked on my act.' Most comics can tell you the best boozers in Edinburgh, but if you ever want to know about tea drinking Brown's your man.

Not everyone in the Assembly Rooms enjoys it. The Vicious Boys once got members of their audience to go to the venue above them and tell the performers to keep the noise down. They did. Mark Steel was in a midnight slot in the Edinburgh Suite in 1988, and he too had problems. 'There was a band next door and above – it was impossible to ignore it. I had to keep referring to it: "There's people trying to get some sleep", "We've got two kids". On the last night the exit door wouldn't close, it kept flying open and people from the street kept poking their heads round the door. These two drunks wandered in, and I sat them down. When Bill Coutts reads this he'll probably try and find out who they were and get them to buy a ticket.'

There was a certain amount of friction – Steel wasn't happy about the place, and let it be known on stage:

'Reading the contract for this place is like the feudal titles that the peasants used to get. I fully expected to find at the bottom something saying we had to look after Bill Coutts' chickens of a Sunday.'

Most comics can tell you the best boozers in Edinburgh, but if you ever want to know about tea drinking Brown's your man

'The contract for this place is like the feudal titles that the peasants used to get'

Opposite: *Simon Fanshawe, Arnold Brown and Liz Lochead (1988)*

126

Coutts didn't only have run-ins with acts without muscle. Fry and Laurie agreed to come, but then had a change of heart.

Coutts: 'I lined them up but then they decided to pull out. One was going to talk at the TV festival and our lawyer threatened that if they didn't fulfil their contract we'd get a sheriff to arrest him while on stage at the TV do. They agreed to do it – but they didn't turn up with a very good show.'

They still easily sold out the Music Hall though.

Television is like a bench-mark for the success of acts. You can be brilliant, but without it you can't easily build a massive audience

Television is like a bench-mark for the success of acts. You can be brilliant, but without it you can't easily build a massive audience. Billy Connolly, of all successful stand-ups in this country, has been the only one really to circumnavigate the waves of telly. The early acts of alternative comedy have dominated the TV medium, first because they are talented but also because they opened the market for themselves. Now acts have to work much harder to get their own series – Julian Clary eventually managed it but only when he had all the force of being one of the most successful live acts in the country behind him.

By 1988 Edinburgh was a professional event for comics and though the social side still went on apace, it had reached middle age. If you wanted to drink late you went to the Gilded Balloon, finished at 3 a.m. and went home. There was the occasional rave somewhere afterwards, but even if you knew about it, the temptation of going home to bed usually won. However there have been some other very pleasant institutions growing up over the years. The best is down to Arthur Smith, who organises regular weekly softball games in the park. They are now also a feature at Clapham Common in London on New Year's Day. Only comics would be mad enough to play softball with a hangover in the middle of the winter and pretend they are having fun.

Smith got a bit adventurous in 1988, and organised a full-blown cricket match. As he organises things, he feels by rights he should win, but unfortunately on this occasion Mark Steel, the opposing captain, knew a journalist who played cricket regularly for the *New Statesman*. He scored a fifty and proceeded to go on and get a lot of wickets – Smith was going to lose. David Tyler, then the producer of *Spitting Image*, went up in the deep to make a catch, fell badly and winded himself. Everyone was very worried, though as he put it afterwards, 'It's not exactly cheering to injure yourself and be surrounded by a mass of comics, making wise-cracks.' Remembering Paul Merton's experience of a few years earlier an ambulance was called. As it appeared thundering over the grass, Smith declared jovially, 'Ambulance stopped play.'

Opposite: *Stephen Fry and Hugh Laurie (1988)*

1989

The Americans are coming. In 1989 there were only three of them at Edinburgh but it may have been the start of a trend. When John Belushi walked into Chicago's 'Second City' impro club in 1971 he was helping found a new-wave of American TV comedy – America's *Comic Strip* ten years before ours. *Saturday Night Live*, which launched Belushi, Dan Ackroyd, Chevy Chase and eventually Eddie Murphy, spurred it on. But the real boom for American stand-up comedy started in 1975. It was the end of the Vietnam War and people wanted to laugh again – be trivial. Enter stage-right the completely-out-to-lunch Steve Martin with his happy feet and stupid tricks, being a Wild and All-Round Crazy Guy. He was to sell albums like a band and play major venues – there was money in this stand-up thing.

What had been till then something of a counter-culture phenomenon suddenly became respectable. There are now hundreds of clubs, comedy chains and business structures across America – stand-up comedy is one of the biggest live art forms there is. It has been claimed that it is actually rivalling rock for bums-on-seats.

Here at Edinburgh in 1989, Emo Philips – 'Comedian and Mammal' as he described himself – was the biggest American success. Already known in London, his weird off-beat character act – a sort of intellectual bum with a sick sense of humour – captured the imaginations of Festival audiences. He sold out the Music Hall easily. What was interesting to see was the panache and domination he had on stage. Except at the top level, very few British acts have it.

In the States Emo Philips is well known but he's no mega-star. Steven Wright, on the other hand, is. On stage he's quiet, doesn't smile and delivers the driest one-liners in the business. They even hype him as 'The Man with the Monotone'. He came over and did a couple of gigs outside the Assembly Rooms complex at the Queen's Hall – not a lot of publicity was needed, every American in town turned up. That's an awful lot of Americans at that time of year.

The third of these tourists had far more in common with the domestic acts. Will Durst is a brilliant satirist which means in America's blander environment he's by no means a major act. At Edinburgh he was one of the hits of the Festival and was nominated for the Perrier.

The British star of the year was Julian Clary. He's the first of the second generation of comics to actually become a national star, now underlined by the success of *Sticky Moments* on Channel 4. He first came up in 1985:

'I was doing the Comedy Boom. It didn't seem like work then; it was parties every night and fun. It gets more like work every year with fewer parties I want to go to. It's also got more insular – no mixing with the hoi-polloi and riff-raff.

'It's different playing in the same room every night. The Music Hall is lovely – the Supper Room dreadful. It smells of old cabbages and the

A weird off-beat character act – a sort of intellectual bum with a sick sense of humour

Opposite: *Gerry Connolly and Doug Tremlett (1988)*

Overleaf: *Emo Philips (1989)*

131

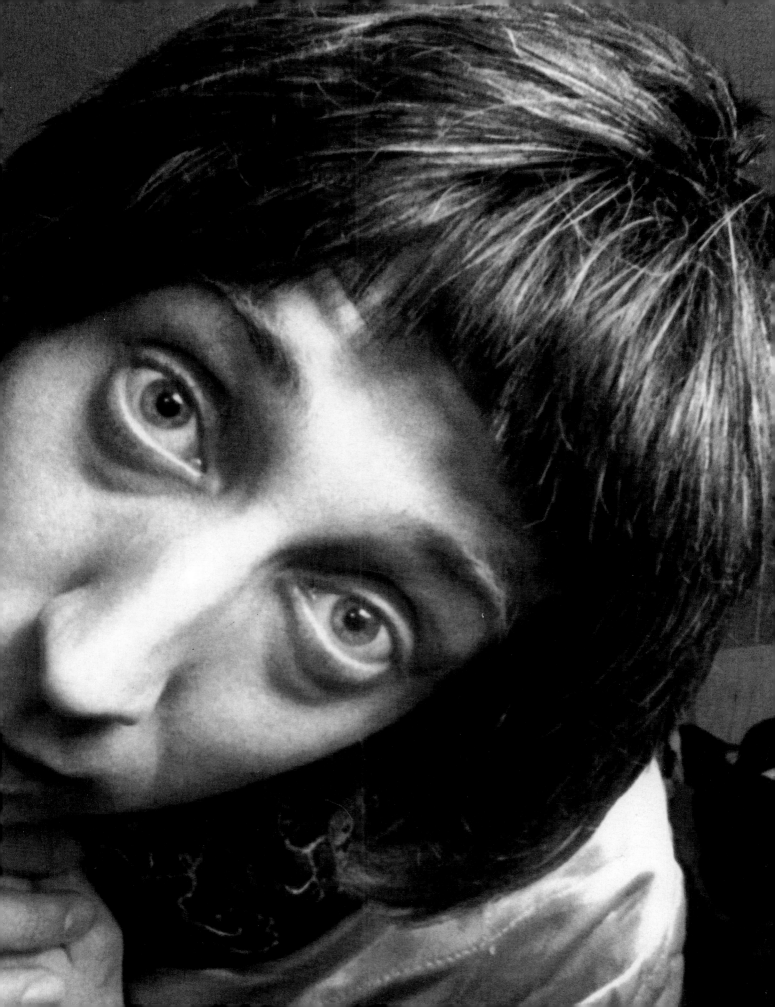

**'It's like being a rabbit on the M4.
After half an hour it affects your brain'**

follow spot is level with your eyes — it's like being a rabbit on the M4. After half an hour it affects your brain.

'By eighty-nine we swanned around letting everyone know we'd arrived. We did the Assembly Rooms and the Gilded Balloon and then weren't seen again till the last night. I much prefer going to the Laughing Duck, a gay bar. It's not so full of theatricals. Well it is, but not ones who've got anything to do with the Fringe.

'I do enjoy Edinburgh but it's not what it was for fun and games. It was friendlier. I sound like some old has-been. These days we make our own fun.'

Stand-up developed with the madness of original rock 'n' roll but slowly and surely it is quietening down. The stakes have risen and with them attitudes have changed.

Clary: 'All the silliness goes. The show becomes more important. At the Comedy Boom you were only talking about making a couple of hundred quid and I was travelling around on my own. Looking back on it it was hard being alone all the time — carrying two suitcases and a dog. I can't think how I did it. Now I travel with others.

'I suppose I miss out by not being on the circuit any more. It used to be quite nice bumping into everyone. But the last time I saw them all the knives were out I can tell you. It's very bitchy these days. I've seen it develop that way over the last five years — it's very hard.'

When Ben Elton turned up to the tenth anniversary of the Comedy Store in 1989 I asked him why he never went to the comedy clubs any more. He replied: 'Cos they all take the piss out of me'

When Ben Elton turned up to the tenth anniversary of the Comedy Store in 1989 I asked him why he never went to the comedy clubs any more. He replied: 'Cos they all take the piss out of me.' He was referring to the other comics. The bitchiness at the Festival that year reached its peak the night Simon Fanshawe won the Perrier Award.

Fanshawe had been a regular at Edinburgh for years. At thirty-two he had finally matured into a strong stand-up. He was always good but it had taken him nearly ten years to really shine on stage. The award was deserved but he certainly didn't win it for being the most popular among his peers. I was one of the judges and that night I lost count of blotchy drunken faces jeering at me: 'How could you do it?' It was like being in one of Hunter S. Thompson's scenarios, with Ralph Steadman doing the graphics.

Fanshawe: 'I was crucified that night. It was bizarre being cold-shouldered for two days. On the night I won *Scotland on Sunday* put John Hegley's picture in the paper saying something like this could be the closest John Hegley gets to winning the Perrier. They had had a tip or something. At the end of my act the paper was thrown on the stage so I could look at it and try and do a gag off the top of it. I saw John's picture

Opposite: *Stephen Wright (1989)*

Overleaf left and right: *Julian Clary (1989)*

135

'I saw the Perrier people in the wings and thought the bastards had come to give me a consolation prize'

and presumed he'd won. Then I saw the Perrier people in the wings and thought the bastards had come to give me a consolation prize.

'The bitchiness is just pressure really. Younger people always bitch about the next generation up. It felt quite good to win the teacher's prize – it's wonderful to be the Benzene Award-winner. The prize was £1500 and chemotherapy for the rest of my life.'

Perrier is the butt of a lot of jokes after their mishap with filters. Still, Nica Burns, the Award's director, maintains: 'Perrier have a sense of humour – they can put up with it,' and comics have always gone on about it being the Bottled Water Award – until they're in the running.

These days comics like Nick Revell are finding new ways to survive the Festival. Revell was back with his one-man satirical show in the Supper Rooms.

'I enjoy the work and try not to socialise the whole time. In fact I enjoy being miserable and anti-social. Conversation gets very repetitive: "How's it going?" "How did you get on?" "Had any good reviews?" "Do you want another drink?" That's why I start chatting about football – to steamroller the shop talk.'

Throughout this book there has been a distinct lack of women. This simply reflects what has been true of comedy generally over the decade but in the last few years it has begun to change. There are more female stand-ups about, and plenty of them are very talented. Although the last female comic to be shortlisted for the Perrier Award was Jenny Lecoat in 1986, more women are filtering through into the Edinburgh system.

Hattie Hayridge is one of them. She started in 1986: 'I'd tried everything else and this seemed to work.' She packed in being a secretary and went off to acting school, then found herself at the Festival under rather weird circumstances.

'I answered an ad on the back of *The Stage* about a show going to the Edinburgh Fringe. I applied and got accepted. But it turned out to be the project of a psychology student who was doing his thesis. He put on a crap play with eight people to see how they'd get on. Of course we didn't get on at all – mind you, when he went home we did. I stayed up after the show finished and that's when I first really started doing open spots. So actually in a funny way he helped me.

'Now I go because otherwise you don't know what you're missing. For me it's like twenty-one New Year's Eve parties on the trot with everything that entails. Good or bad. There are awful New Year's Eves when you want to kill yourself, and there are others that are wonderful. The Festival is the total concentration of twenty-one of those feelings.'

Opposite: *Simon Fanshawe (1989)*

Overleaf left: *Nick Revell (1989)*

Overleaf right: *Hattie Hayridge (1989)*

She was supported in the Assembly Rooms in 1989 by young poetry comic Henry Normal. Hailing from Manchester, Normal represents what may be the beginning of a whole new comedy wave. The cabaret circuit has spread from being solely London-based; most of the major cities of England now have regular comedy clubs. True, a lot of them feed off the talents of the London scene, but home-grown comics are developing in the provinces who can come to London and by no means be out of their depth. It means that you have a chance to learn your trade without having to pack your bags and survive in what is Britain's most expensive city.

A new circuit has also begun to break out in Scotland. STV has showcased it and one Stu Who? even got a few gigs at the Assembly Rooms in 1989.

One of the most satisfying developments of the 1989 Festival was the flowering of poetry comic John Hegley's career. A London circuit act since 1980, everyone in the business rated him highly but until 1989 he had not broken out of the pack. With his first solo show – and a midday slot too – he suddenly found himself a top-line act. It was heart-warming to watch most of his audience stay behind to buy one of his little comedy poetry books and have a word. Hegley is a unique humorist. He doesn't appear to be saying anything much in his silly songs and chats about glasses and dogs, yet somehow he conveys quite complex ideas about what makes us tick and why we act the way we do.

Hegley: 'I was a bit disappointed getting a midday spot at first – then I remembered seeing Jack Klaff [the king of Fringe one-man theatre shows] doing a show at that time. It made me realise that the good thing about it was I could be more theatrical as it wasn't a cabaret time.

'I'm still surprised by the success, that people turn out to see me – it's difficult to believe. I did make an effort to make this happen. People said, Yes, John, you can do twenty minutes – what else is new? I had to move out of that circle, circuit, those circles. I don't play the Store or Jongleurs and that's where people go.

'I really recommend a lunchtime show to anyone. You've got to be careful of getting drunk the night before so it's just the tonic for the binge on the Fringe.

'I was almost happy there this year. I came down to the Assembly Rooms at 11 a.m. And there were the first keen people with their pristine daily diaries spread out in front of them, planning their day. I sat down with a coffee and planned my show with no hangover. Brilliant!'

'I really recommend a lunchtime show to anyone. You've got to be careful of getting drunk the night before so it's just the tonic for the binge on the Fringe'

Opposite: *John Hegley (1989)*

The Scotsman, 19 August, 1989

FRINGE *reviews*

AAAAAAAAAAARGH THE TUNNEL CLUB COMES TO EDINBURGH
Malcolm Hardee
Pleasance

MALCOLM Hardee shambles on stage in an ill-fitting suit looking like a debauched Eric Morecambe and initiaties the funniest show I have seen in Edinburgh this year.

Hardee delivers some gross but hilarious one-liners before giving way to John Maloney, "angry young accordionist": his sharp and aggressive observations had the audience hooting with laughter.

Then Hardee, who looks like he lives in a bus station, introduced the open spot. On the night I went a 13-year-old called Alex Langdon did a stand up routine which put many of his professional elders to shame.

But the highlight of the evening was undoubtedly Terri Rodgers, who walked on looking the epitome of a sweet old lady but then introduced her puppet friend Shorty Harris, who proceeded to tell a string of jokes that made Gerry Sadowitz's material sound like Jimmy Cricket's. This is alternative ventriloquising of the highest order.

William Cook

He'd come up with a really good spoof of the Billy Graham 'Life' poster campaign which had dominated England and Wales – unfortunately it hadn't run in Scotland. All 'UCFK' meant to the locals was he couldn't spell

Things were very straight in 1989 – there were plenty of laughs on stage, but off stage it was business talk as usual. Even Malcolm Hardee was relatively quiet. He'd got the Snakebite Awards going again, which gave him lots of lovely publicity, but it still wasn't helping his show much. He'd called it *Aaaaaaaaargh!! The Tunnel Club Comes to Edinburgh* so it was first in the Fringe programme but that didn't help. He'd come up with a really good spoof of the Billy Graham 'Life' poster campaign which had dominated England and Wales – unfortunately it hadn't run in Scotland. All 'UCFK' meant to the locals was he couldn't spell. Above all, he still hadn't got a review from *The Scotsman*.

In the end the pressure told and he worked out the system for filing copy at *The Scotsman* and decided to file his own review. He had a hangover the morning he was going to sit down and write it so he got another performer to do it for him. It was an excellent spoof of a *Scotsman* review, in fact to be perfectly honest it was far better written than most they print. It worked a treat. The audiences rolled in and *The Scotsman*, though heartily annoyed, refused to give him any more publicity by causing a scene. Hardee was happy and the audiences liked his vulgarity.

Who was the writer? Well, he impressed me so much that I suggested he write the foreword. I think it's reasonably witty for a crap cricketer.

Overleaf: Fabulous Singlettes (1989)

HAVERING
SFC

PERRIER WINNERS

1981: Cambridge Footlights
1982: Writers Inc.
1983: Los Trios Ringbarkus
1984: Brass Band. *Shortlisted*: Fascinating Aida, Hank Wangford Band, Frank Chickens, The Bodgers
1985: Theatre de Complicite. *Shortlisted*: The Bodgers, Merry Mac Fun Show, Paul B. Davies, Sue Ingleton
1986: Ben Keaton. *Shortlisted*: Paul B. Davies, Roy Hutchins, Jenny Lecoat, Merry Mac Fun Show
1987: Brown Blues (Arnold Brown and Barb Jungr and Michael Parker). *Shortlisted*: Nick Revell, Jeremy Hardy, Simon Fanshawe, John Sparkes
1988: Jeremy Hardy. *Shortlisted*: Doug Anthony Allstars, Roy Hutchins, Robert Llewellyn's *Mammon*, The Wow Show
1989: Simon Fanshawe. *Shortlisted*: John Hegley, Al and George, Will Durst, Live Bed Show, The World of Les and Robert

BIBLIOGRAPHY

Berger, Phil, *The Last Laugh: The World of Stand-up Comics*, Limelight Editions, New York, 1986

Hewison, Robert, *Footlights: A Hundred Years of Cambridge Comedy*, Methuen, London, 1984

Wilmut, Roger, *From Fringe to Flying Circus*, Methuen, London, 1982

Wilmut, Roger and Rosengard, Peter, *Didn't You Kill My Mother-in-law?: The Story of Alternative Comedy in Britain from the Comedy Store to Saturday Live*, Methuen, London, 1989

Woodward, Bob, *Wired: The Short Life and Fast Times of John Belushi*, Faber & Faber, London, 1985

PICTURE ACKNOWLEDGEMENTS

Douglas Robertson, photographer for Assembly Theatre Limited.
   Also: Erica Bolton/Jane Quinn (People Show Cabaret), Sean Hudson (Assembly Rooms), Pola Jones Associates (Stephen Fry and Hugh Laurie), Jonathan Littlejohn (Rod Quantock, Julian Clary and Jeremy Hardy), Marc Marnie/Stage-fright Photography (Emo Philips), *Scottish Daily Express* (Gerry Connolly and Doug Tremlett, Rod Quantock and his bus) and Martie Volk (Gerry Sadowitz).

INDEX